COOKING IN
CAJUN
COUNTRY
★ ★ ★

COOKING IN CAJUN COUNTRY

★ ★ ★

Karl Breaux with Cheré Dastugue Coen

GIBBS SMITH

TO ENRICH AND INSPIRE HUMANKIND

Salt Lake City | Charleston | Santa Fe | Santa Barbara

First Edition
09 10 11 12 13   1 2 3 4 5

Published by
Gibbs Smith
P.O. Box 667
Layton, Utah 84041

Orders: 1.800.835.4993
www.gibbs-smith.com

Designed by Debra McQuiston
Printed and bound in the United States
Gibbs Smith books are printed on either recycled, 100% post-consumer waste, FSC-certified papers, or on paper produced from a 100% certified sustainable forest/controlled wood source.

Library of Congress Cataloging-in-Publication Data
Breaux, Karl.
Cooking in Cajun country / Karl Breaux with Cheré Dastugue Coen. — 1st ed.
p. cm.
Includes bibliographical references and index.
ISBN-13: 978-1-4236-0487-7
ISBN-10: 1-4236-0487-3
1. Cookery, Cajun. 2. Cookery, American—Louisiana style. I. Coen, Cheré Dastugue II. Title.
TX715.B837 2009
641.59763—dc22
2008054135

This book is for my Acadian ancestors who not only survived, but thrived after the near annihilation from the great Diaspora of 1755. The Cajun people were granted a new homeland by the Spanish Crown in the form of land grants and a few head of cattle in order to seed Spanish Louisiana with Catholics. The Native American inhabitants of the area helped us by sharing their knowledge of food gathering and natural medicines in this strange new land. The blending of the different cultures that came to Louisiana such as the African, Italian, Lebanese, Sicilian, Creole French, and others created a culinary gestalt of worldwide acclaim.

I thank God that we have managed to preserve our unique culture and French language. May you enjoy the authentic Cajun recipes in this book. Love everybody and have fun, life is short!

—Karl Breaux, a.k.a. Cajun Karl

To Joyce and Penny Dastugue, thanks for the amazing culinary memories.

—Cheré Dastugue Coen

CONTENTS

FOREWORD

"Flavor" is a word that pops up frequently when anyone talks about South Louisiana. We have a "special flavor" in our lifestyle, our music, and even our politics. ✒ But nowhere is the flavor more apparent or more piquante than in the aroma and delicacies that come from the big black iron pots used to simmer and slow cook our traditional foods. ✒ South Louisiana has become justly famous for its Cajun cooking, stirred by Cajun people named Breaux and their kin, but what we call Cajun cooking has roots that predate the arrival of the Acadians in Louisiana. Native Americans and Creoles had an early influence on South Louisiana cooking, introducing ingredients and cooking methods that Cajuns never knew about. ✒ A migration of tens of thousands of people from the West Indies added something new to the pot. So did Spanish, Irish, German, and Italian, and many other cooks who discovered that we can grow delectable fresh herbs alongside the vegetables in our gardens; that there is a natural plenty of crabs, shrimp, and fin fish in our rivers and bayous and the nearby Gulf of Mexico; that the game from our woodlands and wetlands can be cooked up in sauce piquantes and étouffées that have become standard items on our tables. All have contributed a soupçon of this and a pinch of that to the dishes of today.

In many instances, what the world knows as Cajun cooking is something that my Landry and Babin and Vincent grandmothers would never recognize. (Indeed, I once pointed out to Paul Prud-homme, creator of the world-famous blackened redfish dish, that when my grandmother burned the fish, she threw it out.)

But there remain basic ingredients that are necessary for a dish to pass the test—the "holy trinity" of green bell pepper, garlic, and onions, of course, but including some not so tangible ones, such as the patience to properly make a roux or cook on a low and slow fire long enough to bring out every ounce of flavor in a dish.

And that list includes, especially, the ability to season things "just so." I don't know where or how the idea got started that South Louisiana food has to be laced with hot sauce or cayenne pepper that you can barely eat it or taste anything else. Our food is spicy, it is well seasoned, but the heat comes from the cook stove, not from the sauce.

It's that ability to taste a dish, know what's missing and how much of it, and add it to the dish at just the right time that makes all the difference in the world.

There's more to it than mixing the ingredients in a big iron pot with a long wooden spoon. But if you follow these recipes carefully and take your time in doing it, even an amateur can learn to cook so well that just the aroma will cause people to stop in the kitchen, savor the odors, and exclaim, "*Mais là!*"

—Jim Bradshaw, Cajun historian and author

Mais là!

Mais là!

Mais là!

Mais là!

WELCOME TO CAJUN COUNTRY

Travel through South Louisiana and you'll quickly learn that Cajun cooking is more than a heavy dose of black pepper, a splash of tangy hot sauce, or a fancy name to a fast food creation. In fact, much of what the country enjoys as "Cajun" might be as foreign to Louisiana as a snowstorm. Not to mention it's much more delicious. ♦ Cajun cuisine has evolved drastically since the Acadians left the west coast of France for Canada, changing as its people were exiled and relocated to Louisiana, then altered even more when they came in contact with the colony's Spanish, German, Italian, and other nationalities and adopting to the delta's agriculture and livestock. Even in the Cajun heartland of Louisiana, an area that stretches from Mississippi to Texas and incorporates twenty-two parishes (counties), the cuisine differs from region to region. ♦ "Cajun" Karl Breaux, whose family hails back more than two hundred years in South Louisiana, will quickly tell you that nothing goes to waste in a Cajun household, how living off the land was integral to the culture, and how even a day trip out to the camp or houseboat can revive an urban soul. And that from the Mississippi state line to the Sabine River fronting Texas, from the Gulf of Mexico to dead center of the state, Cajuns cook up delectable food in a wide variety of ways. ♦ In this cookbook, Breaux explains the nuances of oyster harvesting in the southeast bayous and the communal tradition of la boucherie, or hog butchering, in the upper prairies. He shows how some areas prefer their gumbos light with seafood while others choose a darker roux with wild game and sausage. Alligator sauce piquante is a favorite along the bayous and marshes while rice dishes dominate the southwest, where crawfish and rice are "grown" in alternating seasons. Crawfish, although consumed statewide, takes on an almost religious significance in Lafayette and surrounding areas, which is why the town of Breaux Bridge is considered the "Crawfish Capital of the World."

Go hunting and fishing with Breaux, who'll share stories as old as the people, and you'll learn why certain foods are so culturally vital to authentic Cajun cooking. Then try them out for yourself.

We hope you enjoy these recipes at home, but please, come visit. The next best thing to reading about Cajun Country and cooking up a gumbo on a chilly fall evening is sampling this unique American cuisine first hand. We'll leave a space at the table.

WHO ARE THE "CAJUNS"?

Before the founding of Jamestown, a group of French pioneers crossed the Atlantic Ocean to settle in what is now the Maritimes region of Canada. Most of their settlements were in Nova Scotia, but some ventured into Prince Edward Island and upper New Brunswick. Because of the massive tides in the Bay of Fundy, these French settlers established fertile farmland by creating an elaborate system of dykes that held back the sea. They called their land *Acadie,* or Acadia.

Over the years these "Acadians" developed a colonial way of life that defined them in language, music, farming, and cuisine. They lived peacefully with the neighboring Indians and rarely participated in the wars between England and France, which had spread into the New World.

Acadie passed back and forth from France to England until the British fully conquered the area in the eighteenth century. The English allowed the Acadians to remain on their land but made demands on their language and Catholic religion, which the Acadians either ignored or attempted to alter through negotiations. Despite being peaceful citizens, the Acadians lived and farmed the richest land in the region and outnumbered the English and were thus viewed as a threat.

Beginning in 1755, in an effort to fully conquer the land and rid Nova Scotia of the "French Neutrals," the English rounded up and deported thousands of Acadians and burned their farms and confiscated their livestock. Families were separated and children lost to their parents. The Acadians were scattered throughout the thirteen American colonies, France, England, the Caribbean, and the Falkland Islands in what became one of the New World's most horrific Diasporas. About half died onboard the ships of disease, exposure, and neglect.

Some Acadians landed in the Catholic areas of Maryland while others were assimilated into English-American society. Some hid out in the woods until they were imprisoned, then bargained their way to Saint Domingue, a French-ruled colony in the Caribbean now known as Haiti. Others managed to return to Nova Scotia but were forced to live on less-sufficient land. Those repatriated to France lived in seaport slums while searching for ways to be independent farmers once again.

When the Acadians heard of a safe haven called Louisiana, which was under Spanish rule at the time, many sought ways to travel to the territory and regroup. Spain was eager to receive more Catholic settlers in an effort to boost the territory's population—and militia—with those friendly to its crown and able to defend it against the British, should they attack. France had originally colonized the Louisiana territory, and even though they were under Spanish control, the residents spoke French. The arriving Acadians were happy to find a language in common with their own.

The first Acadian settlers in Louisiana, in 1765 and 1766, landed in an area along the Mississippi River above New Orleans called St. Jacques de Cabannocé, an area later named the "Acadian Coast." Other Acadian settlements formed in 1766 west of the Mississippi and the Atchafalaya swamp basin in what is now called "Acadiana," including sites that developed into the towns of Lafayette and Opelousas.

The repatriated Acadians in France, with cooperation from the Spanish government, traveled the Atlantic between mid-May and mid-October of 1785, settling in the southwestern region of Louisiana. This last major emigration of Acadians was the largest, at one thousand, five hundred ninety-six people.

Jim Bradshaw, a Lafayette journalist and expert on Acadian history, wrote in *Remembering Our Acadian Heritage*, that, "It would become one of the ironies of our history that more French-speaking settlers would come to Louisiana during the forty years of Spanish rule than during the entire period of French control."

Today, almost a million Acadians live in South Louisiana and another million in the Maritime provinces of Canada.

ACADIAN TO "CAJUN"

In 1803, the Americans arrived in the Louisiana colony with the Louisiana Purchase, and with them the inability to speak French. Hearing "Cadjin" (Cod-jan), which was the French nickname for Acadian (A-ca-dee-an), the Americans called these country residents "Cajuns." Over time, the name stuck.

Today, the title "Acadian" refers to the original inhabitants of the Canadian Maritime Provinces and those descendants who live there today. The Acadians of Louisiana, who are labeled "Cajun," are the only descendants of the original French settlers to that region of Canada, although they are still considered Acadians.

CAJUN VS. CREOLE: WHAT'S THE DIFFERENCE?

Asking a Louisianan the definition of Creole will get you various responses, especially depending on where you're standing. Folks in New Orleans have a few ideas of what Creole means, but that differs from the Creole heritage of Opelousas, home of zydeco in the southwestern part of the state.

On the other hand, Cajun isn't difficult to define, but don't go confusing Cajun cuisine with Creole. Both have origins in French cooking and both tend to be on the spicy side, but typically Creole cuisine is more refined and Cajun more rustic.

Confused? Most people are.

Webster's Dictionary states "Creole" as being "a person of European descent born in the colonies" or "a white person descended from early French or Spanish settlers of the U.S. Gulf states." Other definitions include "a person of mixed French or Spanish and black descent speaking a dialect of French or Spanish."

How does this relate to cuisine? Peter S. Feibleman, author of *American Cooking: Creole and Acadian,* offers a simple explanation:

"The fact is, it (Creole) simply denotes French or Spanish colonists and their descendants, particularly those who maintain some of the customs and language of their mother country. Here in southern Louisiana the original colonists were the French, who began to arrive as early as 1699. Settlers who were Spaniards, Africans, Germans, Italians, and English followed them. Modern Creole cooking reflects nearly all of these—and some other—influences."

When the Acadians came to Spanish Louisiana, their cooking was less refined than their city neighbors, but the colony's French, Spanish, German, and African residents passed on many cooking techniques to the Acadians, such as the use of spices and okra, and sausage-making techniques.

Louisiana residents may simplify the difference between the two cuisines as Creole being a refined cuisine and Cajun the country counterpart. "Creole is to the city as Cajun is to the bayou countryside," writes Kit Wohl in *Arnaud's Restaurant Cookbook.*

New Orleans meals may consist of several courses while a Cajun dinner, such as jambalaya, is created in one pot. Other Cajun standards, which can be quite sophisticated, include boudin sausage, fricassees, or smothered meat over rice, crawfish étouffée, sauce piquante, rice dressing, and all types of fresh seafood boiled, fried, and otherwise.

MCCAJUN AND CREOLE FUSION

Today, both cuisines have evolved into trendy affairs. Creole has been fused with other cuisines by innovative chefs, many of them transplants to New Orleans, to become "contemporary

Creole." Chef Paul Prudhomme made Cajun a household name with his spicy blackened redfish, jalapeño bread, and popcorn crawfish, none of which was traditional in the Cajun home but is now served nationwide as typically Cajun. Unfortunately, Cajun has become synonymous with food that's overly spicy or that originates in New Orleans.

"The only link between corporate America's products and actual Cajun dishes was usually cayenne pepper, which the imitators used to great excess," writes Marcelle Bienvenu, Carl A. Brasseaux, and Ryan A. Brasseaux in *Stir the Pot: The History of Cajun Cuisine.*

THE REAL DEAL

Authentic Cajun cooking includes the "Holy Trinity"—onions, green bell peppers, and celery, ingredients that add flavor to Louisiana meals and do not overpower the senses. Some rather call this infusion the "Four Seasons," which consists of the same three ingredients with garlic thrown in.

Hot sauce and Cajun/Creole seasonings are added to meals depending on the taste of the cook and diners. Louisiana food is flavorful, not mouth scalding.

In a nutshell, Cajun cuisine can best be described as unique, robust with flavor, and down-home good. It's all-American cooking that can be found nowhere else.

Bon appétit!
—Cheré Dastugue Coen

CHAPTER I
★ ★ ★
THE ACADIAN COAST

Upriver from New Orleans lies an agricultural region established during the early days of the Louisiana colony, populated by French and German immigrants seeking a new life. Because of the latter's population, the area was deemed the "German Coast." Around fifty years later, hundreds of Acadian exiles, thrown out of Nova Scotia beginning in 1755, settled upriver as the German farmers had done. This time, however, they settled along the Mississippi River above the original German settlement in an area that would become the "Acadian Coast." As more Acadians entered the area and moved even farther upriver on both sides of the Mississippi, the "Acadian Coast" was renamed the "First Acadian Coast" and the "Second Acadian Coast." The region now encompasses

Attributes that shaped Cajun cooking included African and Native American ingredients such as okra and filé, the Spanish contributions of coffee, chocolate, spice, and beans, and andouille sausage from the Germans. Wild game as well as fresh seafood were incorporated into the cuisine. "You start to see the love of wild food here," Folse said, adding that Cajuns used river shrimp, catfish, garfish, rabbits, squirrels, ducks, frogs, and turtles more often than pork and beef.

the parishes of Ascension, Iberville, St. John the Baptist, West Baton Rouge, and St. Charles according to *Stir the Pot: The History of Cajun Cuisine* by Marcelle Bienvenu, Carl A. Brasseaux, and Ryan A. Brasseaux.

This area along the Mississippi above New Orleans is mainly alluvial farmland with woods, coastal marshes, and wetlands, hosting many different types of crops. Corn became a staple in the Louisiana Acadian diet and rice was a good crop to plant in areas prone to flooding. Vegetables, herbs, and fruits were also grown, enjoying a much longer growing season than the Acadians were used to in Canada.

The Acadian Coast also featured abundant game and fish, allowing the Acadians a ready source of food, particularly in the early lean years of settlement.

Author and television personality Chef John Folse grew up in Ascension Parish and noticed early on the unique blending of cultures in the "River Road" region, an area he describes as an "unbelievable melting pot."

"There's a mélange of techniques and philosophies of cooking in that region that's different from anywhere else," Folse explained. "I think what you're finding here is a mélange of cooking that couldn't have happened in other regions."

Attributes that shaped Cajun cooking included African and Native American ingredients such as okra and filé, the Spanish contributions of coffee, chocolate, spice, and beans, and andouille sausage from the Germans.

Wild game as well as fresh seafood were incorporated into the cuisine. "You start to see the love of wild food here," Folse said, adding that Cajuns used river shrimp, catfish, garfish, rabbits, squirrels, ducks, frogs, and turtles more often than pork and beef.

Because the area relied on sugar cane as a crop and residents had access to the city of New Orleans, sugar and salt became part of the Acadian Coast diet from the 1790s on, he added. Neighboring German dairies provided plentiful eggs and milk. "You start to see sugar as a marinade or poured as a syrup over desserts," Folse said, who added that desserts also included custard pies, cream puffs, floating isles, and rice pudding.

Most desserts were cooked in volume and incorporated leftovers to feed a house full of kids, he said with a laugh, and not necessarily as a treat. "You didn't create a dessert to have something sweet," Folse explained. "It was creating a dessert because you had to get rid of something."

The River Road/Acadian Coast region is home to some of the country's most impressive plantations, including Oak Alley, Laura: a Creole Plantation, and Houmas House. A drive along the Mississippi will reveal one eighteenth century home after another, many that offer tours. Houmas House features the exquisite cooking of Chef Jeremy Langlois of Latil's Landing Restaurant.

Chef Folse serves up his nouveau Cajun cuisine at Lafitte's Landing Restaurant at Bittersweet Plantation, a fine dining restaurant and Bed and Breakfast in Donaldsonville. Bittersweet Plantation Dairy produces products of Cajun and Creole heritage, as well as other nationalities that make up Louisiana. Products include Creole cream cheese, white chocolate praline butter, and a variety of gourmet cheeses.

Belle Rose French Onion Soup

French onion soup on a cold winter night with a glass of Merlot is heavenly. The rich texture of the melted cheese blends in perfectly with the savory beef broth.

2 sticks butter
5 medium onions, julienned
5 tablespoons flour
4 cups beef broth or stock
1 tablespoon beef base
4½ cups water
2 teaspoons Worcestershire sauce
2 teaspoons Cajun/Creole seasoning
1 bay leaf
French bread toast rounds (½-inch thick)
½ cup grated Muenster cheese

MELT BUTTER over low heat in a soup pot. Add the onions and sauté until tender. Do not brown. Add the flour and stir to form a blond roux. Deglaze with beef broth. Add the beef base and stir to completely dissolve. Add the water, Worcestershire sauce, Cajun/Creole seasoning, and bay leaf to pot and let cook uncovered over medium heat for 35 minutes. Remove bay leaf. Serve in soup bowls and top with a piece of French bread toast. Cover toast with cheese.

SERVES 10

Momma's Vegetable Soup

This soup is a must in autumn when the leaves of the pecan trees begin to fall. This soup is pure comfort food and works wonders on a case of the sniffles. A grilled cheese sandwich is the perfect accompaniment to this homemade soup.

3 pounds chuck roast, cut into
   1 x 1-inch chunks
2 pounds soup bones
1 (46-ounce) can V8 juice
2 (15-ounce) cans tomato sauce
1 (4-ounce) can tomato paste
2 cups beef broth
2 tablespoons beef base
3 (15-ounce) cans cream-style corn
2 pounds fresh or frozen whole kernel corn
1 pound fresh or frozen green beans
1 pound fresh or frozen lima beans
1 pound Brussels sprouts
3 tablespoons Cajun/Creole seasoning
1 loaf French bread, optional

PLACE ALL ingredients except the bread in a large soup pot and cook for 2½ hours over medium heat. Remove the soup bones. Serve in soup bowls with toasted French bread, if desired.

SERVES 30

Bayou Goula Prime Rib

This makes a beautiful centerpiece for a glamorous meal—and a happy crowd as well.

1 cup Creole mustard
¾ cup crushed garlic
8-pound rib-eye roast (do not trim fat)
1 (3.4-ounce) bottle Montreal Steak
   Seasoning

PREHEAT OVEN to 450 degrees.

COMBINE THE mustard and garlic. Rub mixture on the roast. Sprinkle the seasoning on the roast to coat. Place on baking pan and bake 20 minutes. Turn oven to 325 degrees and cook for 1 hour and 40 minutes more. Let sit for 15 minutes before carving.

SERVES 8

Mesquite-Crusted Duck

This duck recipe utilizes tamed duck that is moister than its wild cousins because of the fat content. Although the recipe is not complicated, it has a truck-load of flavor.

2 teaspoons Cajun/Creole seasoning
4 teaspoons mesquite-flavored seasoning
1 domestic duck, split in half

PREHEAT OVEN to 350 degrees.

COMBINE THE seasonings and rub all over duck. Place seasoned duck in baking pan and then bake for 75 minutes. Quarter duck and serve on plate with steamed carrots and broccoli, if desired, as a side dish.

SERVES 4

Carville Parmesan Cream Spinach

This decadent side dish is good enough to get a fellow to propose marriage.

8 tablespoons butter, divided
¼ cup flour
Pinch of nutmeg
½ teaspoon Cajun/Creole seasoning
1 cup half-and-half
½ medium onion, diced
2 (10-ounce) packages frozen spinach,
  thawed and liquid squeezed out
¼ cup grated Parmesan cheese

MELT 6 tablespoons butter in a skillet, then add flour, nutmeg, and Cajun/Creole seasoning. Cook for 3 minutes over medium-low heat, whisking constantly. Add half-and-half and stir until sauce is well blended.

IN A separate pan, sauté onion in remaining butter until limp. Add spinach and cook for 5 to 7 minutes, or until tender. Add the cream sauce and Parmesan cheese to spinach. Cook for 2 minutes more, or until cheese is melted. Serve as a side dish.

SERVES 6

Vacherie Chicken Creole

The French word for cattle ranch is *vacherie,* which is where this Louisiana settlement acquired its name. The fertile land and the geographic location of this beautiful place made it an economical location to raise cattle for the region. The chicken Creole recipe served in this area reflects the ingredients that merge New Orleans and Cajun cooking styles.

3 tablespoons cooking oil
3½-pound fryer chicken, cut into 8 pieces
1 medium onion, chopped
1 medium green bell pepper, chopped
1 stalk celery, chopped
1 (15-ounce) can stewed tomatoes
3 teaspoons Cajun/Creole seasoning
2 cloves garlic, chopped
2 cups chicken broth or stock
3 cups water
1 (4-ounce) can tomato paste
1 bunch green onions, chopped
3 cups cooked Louisiana rice

HEAT OIL in a medium Dutch oven. Brown chicken in pot until golden brown. Remove chicken from pot and set aside. Sauté the onion, bell pepper, and celery in pot until tender. Add the tomatoes and Cajun/Creole seasoning and sauté until browning starts. Add the garlic and sauté 3 minutes. Deglaze with broth, scraping bottom of pot to remove any brown bits. Return chicken to pot, add water and tomato paste, and stir, making sure paste is dissolved. Cook, covered, over medium heat for 35 minutes. Uncover and cook 20 minutes more to thicken sauce. Turn off heat. Add green onions and let sit for 10 minutes. Serve over ½ cup cooked rice per serving.

SERVES 6

HOW TO MAKE A ROUX

★ ★ ★

Roux is the basis for much of Cajun cooking, used in gumbos, étouffées, and gravies, among other dishes. The roux is made up of equal parts flour and vegetable oil. In the old days, Cajuns used lard or bacon grease, which produced a more flavorful end product, but cooking oil works well. To create a roux, combine equal parts flour and vegetable oil (or bacon grease or lard) in a heavy gauge pot with a flat surface, such as a cast-iron skillet or Dutch oven. Stir the mixture constantly over high heat, being careful not to burn. Cook the mixture while stirring for 30 to 35 minutes, or until the roux turns a chocolate brown color. For lighter rouxs, use less time; for darker, more. Use the roux immediately or cool and store in the refrigerator for up to 2 months. Bottled manufactured roux is also available in specialty grocery stores and some chain stores. If you purchase bottled roux, follow the directions on the side of the bottle on how to incorporate it into a recipe.

Andouille-Stuffed Pork Loin

I cooked this on a road trip to Arkansas when we were taping an episode of my cooking show in Heber Springs. The locals did not have a chance for conversation once we started eating as they had a mouth full of food until all was gone. I really love visiting our sister state to the north.

16-inch bone-in pork loin
16-inch andouille sausage
3 teaspoons Cajun/Creole seasoning
2 cups water
¼ cup cane syrup

PREHEAT OVEN to 375 degrees.

WITH A long knife, cut an X through the middle of the pork loin. Work the sausage into the hole until the loin is stuffed from side to side. Sprinkle with Cajun/Creole seasoning. Place in a deep pan and then add water. Seal with foil and bake for 3½ hours. Take loin out of pan, drain liquid, and return to pan. Drizzle with cane syrup. Bake at 450 degrees for 8 minutes.

SERVES 12

Saint Joseph Altar Stuffed Artichoke

The stuffed artichoke is an important part of Sicilian culture and was always served on the Saint Joseph feast day.

8 large artichokes
Juice of 1 lemon
4 cups Italian breadcrumbs
3 cups grated Parmesan cheese
1 cup crumbled feta cheese
4 cups extra virgin olive oil
8 lemons, sliced ¼-inch thick
Garlic-flavored olive oil for dipping

PREPARE THE artichokes by cutting off the top third and then cutting the bases so they will sit flat in a pot. Place the trimmed artichokes in a large pot side by side and fill water halfway up the sides of the artichokes. Add lemon juice and cover the pot. Bring water to a slight boil to steam the artichokes for 20 to 25 minutes. Remove from heat. Let cool and place in refrigerator for 1 hour. Remove choke from center of artichoke with fork, being careful not to remove the heart. Combine the breadcrumbs, cheeses, and olive oil in a large mixing bowl.

PREHEAT OVEN to 350 degrees.

FILL THE center cavity of each artichoke with the stuffing mixture and place a little of the stuffing in every leaf of the artichoke using a spoon. Place a slice of lemon on top of each stuffed artichoke and then place on a baking pan. Cover artichokes with aluminum foil and bake for 35 minutes. Uncover and bake for 15 minutes more. Serve with garlic-flavored olive oil on the side for dipping.

SERVES 8

LilyB's Shrimp Creole

Shrimp Creole is one of the dishes that automatically reminds me of the River Road area. I stayed at Tezcuco plantation on River Road when I was courting my wife, Suzanne. Tezcuco burned down a few years ago, but the memory will always live in my mind.

4 tablespoons butter
1 cup chopped onions
1 cup chopped celery
1 small green bell pepper, chopped
2 cloves garlic, minced
Salt and pepper, to taste
½ teaspoon dried basil
2 cups chopped tomatoes or 1 can diced
    tomatoes, with juice
1 pound fresh shrimp, peeled and
    deveined or 2 cups frozen shrimp
½ to 1 cup water
Cajun/Creole seasoning, to taste
2 cups cooked Louisiana rice

MELT BUTTER in a saucepan over medium to medium-high heat. Sauté the onions, celery, and bell pepper until soft, about 5 minutes. Stir in garlic and sauté 5 minutes more. Add salt, pepper, basil, and tomatoes and stir; add shrimp. If using frozen shrimp, add ½ cup water and simmer for 10 minutes. If using fresh shrimp, add shrimp and 1 cup water and simmer until shrimp turn bright pink, about 15 to 20 minutes. Do not overcook. Add Cajun/Creole seasoning to taste. Serve over ½ cup cooked rice per serving.

SERVES 4

Seafood and Artichoke Pasta

This seafood recipe is a must try, making a nice addition to the buffet table during a special event.

2 pounds fettuccine pasta
16 ounces sour cream
1 pound medium Louisiana shrimp, peeled
2 sticks butter, divided
4 teaspoons Cajun/Creole seasoning, divided
1 cup chopped onion
½ cup chopped green bell pepper
½ cup chopped celery
1 pound Louisiana crawfish
1 tablespoon chopped garlic
½ cup flour
1 quart whole milk
2 ounces shrimp powder
1 pound artichoke hearts
1 can (6 ounces) sliced black olives
1 pound smoked or baked catfish
1 pint cherry tomatoes
1 cup grated Parmesan cheese

COOK PASTA according to package directions. Add sour cream and place in a covered dish. Sauté shrimp in skillet with ½ stick butter and season with 1 teaspoon Cajun/Creole seasoning. Pour over pasta, stir, and cover.

IN A deep pot, melt remaining butter and sauté the onion, bell pepper, and celery until soft. Add crawfish and garlic and sauté for 5 minutes. Add flour and stir until a blond roux forms. Add milk and stir, then add shrimp powder, artichoke hearts, olives, and remaining Cajun/Creole seasoning. Cook over medium heat for 10 minutes. Add catfish and tomatoes and cook for 5 minutes more. Pour over pasta mixture and toss with Parmesan cheese.

SERVES 12–14

Donaldsonville Filé Gumbo

The main transportation route for the sugar plantations ran right through the heart of the River Road area. The availability of fresh seafood was staggering as boats traveled from New Orleans to Donaldsonville carrying the wealth of the regional cash crops. The use of filé is prevalent in this area as a thickening agent as well as a flavor enhancer. Be careful—a little goes a long way.

$4\frac{1}{2}$ cups water
$4\frac{1}{4}$ cups seafood stock
1 cup roux (see page 28)
1 large onion, chopped
1 small green bell pepper, chopped
4 teaspoons Cajun/Creole seasoning
1 pound medium shrimp,
  peeled and deveined
1 pint shucked oysters, with
  oyster liquid
2 teaspoons filé
3 cups cooked Louisiana rice

BRING WATER and stock to a boil in a large soup pot. Add roux and stir until completely dissolved. Add onion, bell pepper, and Cajun/Creole seasoning, and cook uncovered over medium heat for 1 hour. Add the shrimp and cook for 15 to 20 minutes. Add the oysters with liquid and turn off heat. Let sit for 15 minutes. Add filé and stir to incorporate into gumbo. The gumbo will thicken rapidly. Serve in soup bowls over $\frac{1}{2}$ cup cooked rice per serving.

SERVES 6

St. Gabriel Beef and Mushroom Rice

On one of my trips to tape a TV episode in Arkansas, I was fortunate enough to happen upon a shiitake mushroom farm. The owners shared some of the flavorful fungi with me and this is a recipe I created. This rice dish will make you a hero with your friends!

4 tablespoons butter, divided
⅔ cup diced shiitake mushrooms, rehydrated
1 cup sliced button mushrooms
½ cup chopped onion
¼ cup chopped green bell pepper
¼ cup chopped celery
2 tablespoons chopped garlic
1 cup shiitake mushroom stock*
1 teaspoon Cajun/Creole seasoning
1 tablespoon beef base
¼ cup chopped green onions
2½ cups cooked Louisiana rice

MELT 2 tablespoons butter in a large skillet and sauté the mushrooms over high heat to brown. Add the onion, bell pepper, celery, and garlic, and sauté until onions are transparent. Deglaze with the stock, season with Cajun/Creole seasoning, and add beef base. Cook for 10 minutes over medium heat. Turn off heat and add the green onions and remaining butter. Incorporate the cooked rice and stir well.

SERVES 6

*MAKE THE stock from placing dehydrated shiitake mushrooms in hot water to reconstitute and then use the resulting liquid.

Plaquemine Lock Crawfish Rice Dressing

Cajun rice dressing is also called "dirty rice" because of the beef. Outside of Cajun country, it is served at meals as the starch, but this recipe can also be served as the main course.

1 pound dressing mix (a combination stuffing mix with ground chicken liver and ground chicken gizzard found in the frozen section)
1 pound ground beef
½ cup chopped onion
¼ cup chopped green bell pepper
¼ cup chopped celery
2 tablespoons chopped garlic
2 teaspoons Cajun/Creole seasoning
1¼ to 1½ cups chicken broth
1½ tablespoons dark roux (see page 28)
1 pound Louisiana crawfish tails
2 (10.5-ounce) cans cream of celery soup
8 cups cooked Louisiana rice
1 bunch green onions, chopped

LIGHTLY BROWN dressing mix and ground beef together. Add onion, bell pepper, celery, garlic, and Cajun/Creole seasoning, and sauté until vegetables are limp. Add broth, then dissolve the roux in pot. Add the crawfish tails and condensed celery soup, mix and let cook over medium heat for 25 to 30 minutes. Remove from heat, stir in cooked rice and green onions and serve.

SERVES 12

River Road Pralines

Don't think about calories when you make these sweet delicacies. It's a waste of time.

2 cups sugar
1 cup light brown sugar
Pinch of salt
1 cup evaporated milk
4 tablespoons butter
2 cups pecan pieces

MIX SUGARS, salt, milk, and butter over medium-high heat in a large saucepan, stirring frequently. When the mixture reaches the soft-ball stage on a candy thermometer (234 degrees), remove from heat and whip with a wire whisk until creamy, about 10 to 15 minutes, or until mixture becomes thick enough to create small patties. Add pecans and stir until mixed adequately, and then drop by spoonfuls onto waxed paper. Allow to cool at room temperature. Can be eaten as pralines or crumbled to top of vanilla ice cream.

MAKES ABOUT 12 LARGE OR 24 SMALL PRALINES

CHAPTER 2 ★ THE WETLANDS

Some of the Cajuns who settled along the Mississippi River upon entering Louisiana began migrating down Bayou Lafourche, a long drainage of Mississippi River water that wound its way for miles to the Gulf of Mexico. In French, *lafourche* means the fork, and was so named for its divergence from the Mississippi. Towns along the bayou include the French-named Paincourtville, Napoleonville, and Labadieville. Southwest of the river settlements, skirting the Atchafalaya swamp basin, rose up Cajun towns such as Bayou Goula, Bayou Sorrel, and Pierre Part, where French is widely heard today. As Cajuns moved into new lands, they traveled farther south along Bayou Lafourche until they reached the Gulf of Mexico. Residents settled along the rich soils of the bayou and, like the

The largest town along the bayou is Thibodaux, home of the Wetlands Acadian Cultural Center of the Jean Lafitte National Historical Park and Preserve. The museum contains information on Acadian culture, religion, cuisine, recreation, and industry through exhibits and films, in addition to changing exhibits and demonstrations of Cajun culture, such as boat building, net making, and food preparation. Local musicians perform Monday evenings and Sunday afternoons in jam sessions where residents visit and dance the two-step and traditional Cajun waltz.

Mississippi River plantations and farms, placed their homes near the bayou and farmed land that stretched far back from the waterway.

Towns that emerged along the bayou tended to be horizontal, with homes up one side and down the other. Before bridges were built, Cajuns visited each other by horseback if they lived on the same side of the bayou or by pirogue (a Cajun style of canoe) if they needed to visit others across the water.

Because of this settlement pattern that stretched about 110 miles down Bayou Lafourche, the waterway has been called "the longest street in the world." Bayou Lafourche meets the Gulf at Port Fourchon, an oil and gas industrial terminal and a fisherman's saltwater haven where many Cajuns have camps for weekend outdoor recreation.

The largest town along the bayou is Thibodaux, home of the Wetlands Acadian Cultural Center of the Jean Lafitte National Historical Park and Preserve. The museum contains information on Acadian culture, religion, cuisine, recreation, and industry through exhibits and films, in addition to changing exhibits and demonstrations of Cajun culture, such as boat building, net making, and food preparation. Local musicians perform Monday evenings and Sunday afternoons in jam sessions where residents visit and dance the two-step and traditional Cajun waltz.

Farther south in Terrebonne Parish lies the town of Houma, named after the area's Native American tribe. In Houma, Cajun

culture and the seafood industry are represented at the Bayou Terrebonne Waterlife Museum, and the surrounding area offers great fishing opportunities from both salt and fresh water sources and breathtaking swamp tours. The local seafood industry boasts of jumbo Gulf shrimp, oysters, crabs, and a wide variety of fish such as trout, redfish, cobia, snapper, and tuna, to name only a few.

Cajun cuisine of the wetlands incorporates much of the fresh seafood readily available and abundant to residents. Culinary styles indicative of this area include typical Cajun dishes, and some include pastas, due to the influx of Italian immigrants in the early twentieth century. Creole cooking has also influenced the modern culinary landscape due to the easy proximity to New Orleans.

One of the tragedies of southeast Louisiana has been its massive loss of wetlands, which disappear at the rate of one football field an hour. Houma blues musician Tab Benoit created the Voice of the Wetlands, a volunteer-led organization dedicated to raising awareness of wetlands and coastal land loss. Every fall Benoit hosts the Voice of the Wetlands Festival on the grounds of Houma's Southdown Plantation. It is a fête that includes the best names in Cajun and zydeco music and some of the finest Cajun food around.

Other annual food fêtes include the Louisiana Catfish Festival in Des Allemands, the Bon Mangé Festival in Gheens, and the Louisiana Gumbo Festival in Chackbay.

Bayou Vista Seafood Gumbo

The use of tomatoes and ham in this region of Acadiana produces a unique tasting gumbo. The availability of fresh Gulf shrimp and blue point crabs practically year-round ensures a quality end product. The stock can be made by boiling the shrimp peelings in water for 45 minutes and straining the resulting broth. It can then be frozen and used when needed.

8 cups water
2 cups shrimp or seafood stock
¼ cup roux (see page 28)
1 (4-ounce) can tomato paste
1 (4-ounce) can tomato sauce
6 whole crabs, cleaned
2 medium onions, chopped
1 green bell pepper, chopped
2 cloves garlic, chopped
2 bay leaves
2 pounds okra, sliced ¼-inch thick
1 pound smoked ham, cut into
    1-inch cubes
2 tablespoons Cajun/Creole seasoning
2 pounds medium shrimp, cleaned
    and deveined
1 pound crabmeat (claw)
1 quart oysters, with liquid
1 bunch green onions, chopped
5 cups cooked Louisiana rice

BRING THE water and stock to a boil in a large soup pot. Add the roux, tomato paste, and tomato sauce; stir to dissolve. Add the whole crabs, onions, bell pepper, garlic, bay leaves, okra, ham, and Cajun/Creole seasoning. Cook over medium heat for 45 minutes. Add shrimp, crabmeat, and oyster liquid and cook over medium heat for 25 minutes. Remove soup pot from heat. Add oysters and green onions. Remove the bay leaves before serving. Spoon into soup bowls over ½ cup cooked rice per serving.

SERVES 10

Montegut Crab Stew

Along the bayous of this part of Cajun Country you will find shrimp boats parked next to people's homes. Many Cajuns in this beautiful coastal region make a living off the sea. The sides of the roads are home to crab stands where you can purchase huge blue point crabs for great prices.

8 cups water
4¼ cups seafood stock (can substitute canned clam broth)
2 cups roux (see page 28)
12 whole crabs, cleaned
2 medium onions, chopped
1 large green bell pepper, chopped
1 stalk celery, chopped
1 (10-ounce) can Rotel tomatoes
2½ teaspoons Cajun/Creole seasoning
2 bay leaves
1 pound crabmeat (claw)
1 pound lump crabmeat
1 bunch green onions, chopped
6 cups cooked Louisiana rice

IN A large soup pot, bring water and stock to a boil. Add roux and stir until completely dissolved. Be careful not to add too fast as the liquid may overflow. Add the whole crabs, onions, bell pepper, celery, tomatoes, Cajun/Creole seasoning, and bay leaves to pot and cook over medium heat for 1 hour. Add the crabmeat and cook 10 minutes; remove from heat. Remove bay leaves. Add green onions and serve in soup bowls over ½ cup cooked rice per serving.

SERVES 12

Theriot Sausage–Stuffed Ducks

The duck hunting in this part of Acadiana is legendary. In the winter months people pay up to $1,000 per person a day to hunt with guides. Getting a day's limit is done sometimes in a hour. The Mandarin oranges complement the gravy and tame the wild duck taste.

2 pounds fresh pork sausage
1 (10-ounce) can Mandarin oranges,
    juice reserved
4 teal ducks, cleaned
5 slices bacon, chopped
1 large onion, sliced
1 green bell pepper, sliced
2 tablespoons flour
1 (15-ounce) can beef broth
1 (12-ounce) can beer
2 teaspoons Cajun/Creole seasoning
½ bunch green onions, chopped
½ to ⅔ cup cooked Louisiana rice
    per serving

MIX THE sausage and Mandarin oranges together and stuff the cavity of the ducks with the mixture. Sauté the bacon until crisp in a medium Dutch oven; remove bacon.

BROWN THE ducks in the bacon grease until golden brown; remove ducks. Sauté the onion and bell pepper in the bacon grease until tender. Stir in the flour and whisk until a roux forms. Deglaze with the beef broth and beer. Return ducks to pot; add the Cajun/Creole seasoning, bacon, and reserved juice and cook, covered, over medium heat for 90 minutes. Remove from heat and add green onions. Serve on bed of cooked rice.

SERVES 4

Chauvin Oyster Soup

I have been fishing in the Dulac area all of my life at a camp about a mile from Wilson's Oysters. My buddies and I always purchase a couple of sacks of oysters and put some beer on ice. We eat until we are stuffed and still end up with a couple gallons of this freshly caught treasure of the sea. The next day I always prepare this awesome soup and share it with family and friends.

1 medium onion, very finely chopped
1 stick butter
¼ cup flour
2 cups heavy cream
2 cups milk
3 teaspoons Cajun/Creole seasoning
¼ teaspoon nutmeg
¼ teaspoon Cajun-style hot sauce
1 quart oysters, with oyster liquid
½ bunch green onions, chopped
1 loaf French bread, optional

SAUTÉ ONION in butter in a soup pot over low heat until tender. Add flour and stir over medium heat until a blond roux forms. Add heavy cream and milk and stir to mix with roux. Cook over medium heat for 5 to 7 minutes; the sauce will thicken rapidly. Add the Cajun/Creole seasoning, nutmeg, hot sauce, and oyster liquid. Cook the soup for 15 to 20 minutes over medium heat. Remove from the heat and add the oysters and green onions. Serve in soup bowls with crusty French bread on the side, if desired.

SERVES 4

Bayou Cane White Bean Soup with Pasta

We are fortunate to have had a large group of Sicilians settle in South Louisiana. These hard-working Italians introduced their cooking methods to the Acadians, which is evidenced here in this take on Pasta Fazool.

2 pounds salt pork, cut into 1-inch cubes
2 medium onions, chopped
1 medium green bell pepper, chopped
1 stalk celery, chopped
2 tablespoons cooking oil
2 cloves garlic, chopped
1 gallon water
3¾ cups chicken broth or stock
1 (15-ounce) can stewed tomatoes,
   including liquid
4 teaspoons Cajun/Creole seasoning
1 pound dried great Northern beans
1 pound medium shrimp,
   peeled and deveined
1 pound macaroni pasta
1 bunch green onions, chopped

IN A medium-size pot, sauté the salt pork, onions, bell pepper, and celery in oil until the vegetables are tender and the meat starts to brown. Add the garlic and sauté for 3 minutes. Add the water, broth, tomatoes, Cajun/Creole seasoning, and beans. Bring to a boil for 20 minutes, then lower to medium heat and cook, covered, for 1½ hours. Add shrimp and pasta to pot and cook over medium heat for 25 minutes more. Turn off the heat and add the green onions. Serve in soup bowls.

SERVES 10

Aunt Cleo's Oyster Patties

Oysters are an expensive delicacy for most people in the world, but here it is still possible to purchase a 144-count sack for $20. In the winter, people often buy a sack and go hog wild.

½ dozen patty shells (frozen puff pastry shells)
2 dozen oysters, in oyster liquid
1 tablespoon butter or margarine
1 small onion, grated
1 tablespoon flour
½ (4-ounce) can chopped mushrooms and juice
½ teaspoon salt
½ teaspoon pepper
½ teaspoon cayenne pepper
¼ teaspoon lemon juice

COOK PASTRY shells according to directions.

MEANWHILE, COOK oysters in their own liquid, bring to a boil, then simmer 10 minutes. Melt butter in a saucepan, add onion and blend in flour until smooth. Add ½ cup mushroom juice, salt, pepper, cayenne, and mushrooms. Add oysters and lemon juice. Cook 5 minutes, then pour into patty shells. Bake at 400 degrees for 12 to 15 minutes.

SERVES 6

Lake Boudreaux Chicken Sauce Piquante

Boudreaux's Marina in Cocodrie, Louisiana, is at the very end of Highway 56. The availability of different types of seafood here is incredible. I usually like to cook a good chicken sauce piquante for my fishing buddies after a few days of crab, shrimp, and fish.

4 tablespoons cooking oil
6-pound chicken, cut into 12 pieces
2 large onions, chopped
2 medium green bell peppers, chopped
1 stalk celery, chopped
1 (4-ounce) can tomato paste
1 (10-ounce) can Rotel tomatoes
2 cloves garlic, chopped
3¾ cups chicken broth or stock
6 cups water
1 (15-ounce) can tomato sauce
4 teaspoons Cajun/Creole seasoning
½ teaspoon Cajun-style hot sauce
2 teaspoons pickling spice, wrapped
   in cheesecloth and tied to form
   a bouquet garni
1 bunch green onions, chopped
1 bunch parsley, chopped
4 cups cooked Louisiana rice

HEAT OIL in a large Dutch oven. Add cut hen to pot and brown on all sides until golden brown. Remove from pot and set aside. Add onions, bell pepper, and celery to pot and sauté until tender. Add tomato paste and brown for about 10 minutes over medium-high heat, stirring often. Add tomatoes and cook until the mixture starts to thicken. Add garlic and sauté for 5 minutes more.

DEGLAZE BOTTOM of pot with broth, scraping bottom to release brown bits. Return chicken to pot. Add water, tomato sauce, Cajun/Creole seasoning, hot sauce, and pickling spice to pot. Cook over medium heat for 2½ hours. Remove bouquet garni. Sauce will have thickened considerably. Remove from heat and add the green onions and parsley. Serve on plates over ½ cup cooked rice per serving.

SERVES 8

Boston Canal Backstrap

Venison is consumed in Cajun Country as a regular dinner item, as much as beef and pork. The backstrap, or tenderloin, is reserved for special dishes such as this, nicely served with a good bottle of Cabernet Sauvignon.

1 (8-ounce) package cream cheese, cut
  into 8 equal slices
8 venison loin steaks, butterflied
16 (⅛-inch-thick) slices onion
16 (⅛-inch-thick) slices green bell pepper
8 (¼-inch thick) slices jalapeño
3 teaspoons Cajun/Creole seasoning
16 slices smoked bacon

PLACE CREAM cheese slices in freezer for 45 minutes. Place venison steaks on a flat surface. Place 2 slices onion, 2 slices bell pepper, 1 slice jalapeño, and 1 slice cream cheese on each steak. Roll each steak up and season liberally with Cajun/Creole seasoning. Wrap two slices bacon around each rolled-up steak. Secure with toothpicks. Grill over medium-high heat until bacon crisps and the meat is medium-rare. Serve as appetizer or main meat dish.

SERVES 8

Port Fourchon Crab and Shrimp Rice

Port Fourchon, Louisiana, is a haven for fishermen in Acadiana. With so many species of fish, crustaceans, and shellfish available, it is a destination point for serious anglers. This recipe is perfect for a Lenten Friday meal.

1 pound small peeled shrimp
1 pound crabmeat (claw)
6 cups cooked Louisiana rice
1 bunch green onions, chopped
1 stick butter
½ cup chopped yellow onions, sautéed
2 teaspoons Cajun/Creole seasoning

PLACE ALL ingredients in a large mixing bowl and stir until well mixed. Place in an aluminum baking bag (can be homemade) and place on a hot pit for 20 to 25 minutes, turning a couple of times. Check for doneness and serve.

SERVES 8

Galliano Eggplant/Shrimp Cornbread Dressing

The residents grow lush vegetable gardens along the banks of the Houma waterways such as Bayou Terrebonne and Bayou Du Large in the rich alluvial soil. There are few places in the United States that consume as much eggplant as we Cajuns do. This type of cornbread dressing is served at special gatherings such as Christmas or Easter.

4 pounds eggplant
2 tablespoons cooking oil
$1/2$ cup water
4 teaspoons Cajun/Creole seasoning, divided
1 pound ground pork
1 pound ground beef
1 (10.75-ounce) can cream of shrimp soup
2 (10.75-ounce) cans cream of celery soup
1 pound medium Louisiana shrimp
1 cube fish bouillon
2 pans of cornbread (10 x 12-inches each), cooled and crumbled
$1^1/2$ cups chicken broth or stock

PREHEAT OVEN to 350 degrees.

COARSELY CHOP the eggplant into pieces in a food processor. In a large heavy frying pan, sauté chopped eggplant in the oil, with the water and 2 teaspoons Cajun/Creole seasoning, over medium heat for 35 minutes; stir often and then remove from the pan. In the pan, brown the pork and beef. Add cooked eggplant mixture and condensed soups. Cook over low heat for 5 minutes. Place mixture aside, then sauté shrimp until pink. Add fish bouillon and stir well. Add to the eggplant mixture. Add remaining Cajun/Creole seasoning, cornbread, and broth. Mix well and place in a large baking dish (about 20 x 14 inches) and then bake for 45 minutes.

SERVES 16

Cut Off Smothered Mustard Greens

Cut Off, Louisiana, is a small community on the way to Grand Isle. It seems that everyone is either from there or related to someone who is. The friendly folks who live in Cut Off are fiercely proud of their heritage. The cooking of mustard greens in the winter was a result of it being available in the garden at that time of year.

½ pound smoked sausage, cut into
  ½- to 1-inch pieces
6 tablespoons water
1 tablespoon chicken base
3 cans (16 ounces each) mustard
  greens, drained
1½ teaspoons Cajun/Creole seasoning

BROWN SAUSAGE over medium heat for 5 minutes; deglaze with water. Add chicken base and stir well. Add the mustard greens to pot along with Cajun/Creole seasoning. Cook for 30 minutes over medium-low heat.

SERVES 8

Lost Lake Barbecue Redfish

Redfishing is some fun; this species of fish hits the bait with a furious temper. The joy of fighting with the fish is as good as the delightful flavor of the meat. If you get a chance to experience redfishing, go for it!

6 (1½-inch-thick) redfish fillets, skins on
3 sticks butter
1 teaspoon garlic powder
3 tablespoons Worcestershire sauce
1 teaspoon Cajun-style hot sauce
4 tablespoons lemon juice
3 teaspoons Cajun/Creole seasoning

SCORE FISH fillets in a diamond pattern, about 1-inch squares. Melt butter in a saucepan over low heat. Add the garlic powder, Worcestershire sauce, hot sauce, lemon juice, and Cajun/Creole seasoning and stir to blend. Place the fillets skin side down on a hot grill and baste with the butter mixture frequently until meat is firm and separates from the skin. Remove from grill and serve on plates skin side down.

SERVES 6

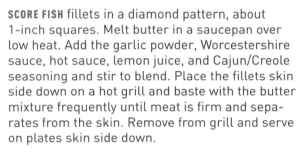

Caillou Lake Pork Chops with Fig Gravy

This unusual combination of two wonderful ingredients produces unforgettable gravy.

8 center-cut pork chops, 3/4-inch thick
3 tablespoons cooking oil
2 medium onions, julienned
1 medium green bell pepper, julienned
2 cups chicken broth or stock
1 tablespoon beef base
2½ teaspoons Cajun/Creole seasoning
3/4 cup fig preserves (available in most
  supermarkets in the jelly section)
½ stick butter
4 cups cooked Louisiana rice

IN A medium Dutch oven, brown the pork chops in oil on both sides until golden brown; remove meat and set aside. Sauté onions and bell pep-per until tender. Add the broth, beef base, and Cajun/Creole seasoning. Stir to dissolve the beef base and cook, covered, over medium heat for 45 minutes. Add preserves and cook, uncovered, for 10 minutes. Remove from heat and add butter to sauce 1 tablespoon at a time; stir to dissolve after each addition. Serve on plates over ½ cup cooked rice per serving.

SERVES 8

Nicholls State Eggplant Feta Wheels

Thibodaux, Louisiana, is the crossroads area where different cultures of southern Acadiana intertwine. The Sicilians in this part of the state heavily influenced the cuisine. The recipe below is guaranteed to be a crowd pleaser.

1 large eggplant, cut into 8 (½-inch thick) slices
3 tablespoons olive oil
1 teaspoon Cajun/Creole seasoning
8 tomato slices, cut about ½-inch thick
8 ounces crumbled Feta cheese

PLACE A 16-inch sheet of aluminum foil on a hot barbecue pit, crimping the edges. Place eggplant on foil and drizzle with about half of the oil and Cajun/Creole seasoning. Cook until eggplant is tender, about 15 to 20 minutes. Place a tomato slice on top of each eggplant slice and add more oil and seasoning. Cover with cheese and cook until cheese melts. Serve immediately.

SERVES 4

Bread Pudding

The most popular dessert in Cajun Country—and South Louisiana—is bread pudding. With this recipe, you have the option of including raisins.

3 eggs
1 (12-ounce) can evaporated milk
½ cup whole milk
1 teaspoon vanilla
1 teaspoon cinnamon
1 teaspoon nutmeg
1 cup sugar
4 cups cubed stale French bread, cut into 1-inch cubes
1 cup raisins (optional)

PREHEAT OVEN to 350 degrees.

WHISK THE eggs, then add the milks, vanilla, cinnamon, and nutmeg and mix well. Add the sugar and mix well. Place the French bread with the raisins in a 9 x 9 x 2-inch greased pan, covering the bottom. Pour egg and milk mixture over the bread and raisins, making sure bread is thoroughly soaked and covered. Bake for 45 minutes.

SERVES 8

CHAPTER 3: UPPER PRAIRIE

After being deported from Nova Scotia and sent into exile, Acadians began migrating to the Spanish colony of Louisiana in 1757, according to Carl Brasseaux in *The Founding of New Acadia.* Approximately one thousand Acadians had entered the colony by 1770. Several of these early Acadians headed west over the Atchafalaya Basin, the nation's largest river drainage swamp, and into areas that are now the cities of Lafayette and Opelousas. The oldest town in the Upper Prairie region is Opelousas, the third oldest city in Louisiana, founded in 1720 as a military post and trading station with the Opelousas Indians. "Le Poste des Opelousas" attracted various nationalities, including Acadians, Napoleonic refugees, and aristocratic French Creoles.

Eunice is also home to Savoy's Music Center, where owner and accordion maker Marc Savoy and his wife, Ann, host Saturday morning Cajun music jam sessions that are famous worldwide. The Savoys perform as a family in the Savoy Family Band. Ann Savoy performs in her own band and occasionally with Linda Rondstadt, Michael Doucet, and other notable musicians. And that's only the tip of the iceberg of this incredibly talented family.

Over time, Cajuns settled further west, creating the towns of Eunice with its long Cajun musical history, Mamou with its famous Cajun Mardi Gras, and the Ville Platte area with its tradition of smoked meats.

Fertile farmlands dot the Upper Prairie region with rice and crawfish ponds, while the lush grass provides a perfect feast for cattle and other livestock. Smoked meats are a trademark of the upper western region of Cajun Country.

"The area is perhaps best known for its rice-and-pork-based white boudin and smoked meats," writes Marcelle Bienvenu, Carl A. Brasseaux, and Ryan A. Brasseaux in *Stir the Pot: The History of Cajun Cuisine.* "Rice, braised beef, and brown gravy are the staples of the diet here . . ."

Louisiana produces about fifteen percent of the United States' yams, and the sweet root vegetable is used in many dishes in Cajun cooking, whether served alone and topped with cane syrup and cinnamon or sliced and fried or used in pies. Opelousas celebrates its fall yam harvest with the Louisiana Yambilee Festival.

In Eunice, at the Prairie Acadian Cultural Center of the Jean Lafitte National Historical Park and Preserve, demonstrations are routinely held on Cajun cooking, as well as weaving fabric and creating musical instruments. The museum tells the story of the prairie Cajuns through exhibits and award-winning films and hosts a weekly live radio show, *Rendezvous des Cajuns,* at the historic Liberty Theatre featuring Cajun and zydeco music.

Eunice is also home to Savoy's Music Center, where owner and accordion maker Marc Savoy and his wife, Ann, host Saturday morning Cajun music jam sessions that are famous worldwide. The Savoys perform as a family in the Savoy Family Band. Ann Savoy performs in her own band and occasionally with Linda Rondstadt, Michael Doucet, and other notable musicians, and Joel Savoy is part owner of Valcour Records, promoting Louisiana musicians. And that's only the tip of the iceberg of this incredibly talented family. Their story repeats itself throughout South Louisiana, proving that the region boasts of some of the finest musicians in the country.

In South Louisiana, it's a rare home that doesn't include Tony Chachere's Original Creole Seasoning on its table. The unique blend of spices have livened up many a home-cooked meal, from adding flavor to gumbos and étouffées to spicing up home fries. The company also produces a line of dinner mixes, sauces, marinades, and rouxs at its Opelousas factory.

Savoie's began as a small grocery in 1949 by Eula and Tom Savoie in rural St. Landry Parish and today produces a wide variety of "real Cajun" food products such as smoked sausage, andouille, tasso, roux, hogshead cheese, and dressing mixes.

Other products produced in the Upper Prairie include Slap Ya Mama seasoning blends and Kary's bottled roux, both of Ville Platte.

Pecanierre Pork Chops

Hog lard is the magic of this recipe. It is not easy to find, so you can substitute cooking oil. In the old days, bacon grease and lard were the only forms of oil available in South Louisiana. These fried pork chops should be eaten soon after cooking as the lard used in the cooking process gets a rancid taste if left over for the next day.

4 eggs, beaten
1 (12-ounce) can evaporated milk
4 tablespoons mustard
1 teaspoon red hot sauce
1 teaspoon green hot sauce
10 ($\frac{1}{2}$-inch) center-cut pork chops
3 cups self-rising flour
3 tablespoons Cajun/Creole seasoning
1 gallon hog lard (or substitute peanut oil)

IN A large bowl, mix the eggs, milk, mustard, and hot sauces. Place pork chops in a large plastic bag and then pour mixture into bag and let marinate for at least 30 minutes. In another plastic bag, place the flour and Cajun/Creole seasonings; mix together. Place marinated pork chops in flour bag, two at a time, and shake until well coated. Remove from the bag. Fry in lard in a deep fryer until golden brown and serve.

SERVES 10

Grand Mary Chuck Steak Gumbo

The fertile soil of St. Landry Parish enabled ranchers to raise cattle at an economical rate. The bayous of the area allowed access to the commercial meat markets of New Orleans and St. Louis. The Cajuns and Creoles of this area had plenty of beef on hand and developed wonderful ways of cooking it. This gumbo uses the chuck roast that is perfect for this braising method.

3 pound chuck steaks, cut into
  3-inch cubes
3 tablespoons cooking oil
2 medium onions, chopped
1 large green bell pepper, chopped
1 stalk celery, chopped
2 cloves garlic, chopped
3 teaspoons Cajun/Creole seasoning
2 cups beef broth
1½ gallons water
1 cup dark roux (see page 28)
2 teaspoons beef base
1 bunch green onions, chopped
1 bunch parsley, chopped
6 cups cooked Louisiana rice

BROWN CHUCK steak cubes on all sides in oil in a heavy soup pot over medium-high heat. Cook until a rich brown color. Add onions, bell pepper, and celery, and sauté until soft; stir often. Add garlic and Cajun/Creole seasoning and sauté for 3 to 5 minutes. Do not burn garlic. Deglaze with broth and water, scraping the bottom of the pot to dissolve the brown particles formed in the searing process. Bring liquid to a boil and add the roux and beef base, stirring constantly to dissolve. Cook the gumbo, uncovered, over medium heat for 1½ hours. Turn off heat and add the green onions and parsley. Serve in soup bowls over ½ cup cooked rice per serving.

SERVES 12

Bunkie Yellow Squash

The mild climate of Louisiana allows year-round gardening of vegetables, tubers, and roots. Many people are raised eating whichever vegetable was in season. This is a favorite dish from the backyard garden.

1½ sticks butter, divided
1 small yellow onion, diced
3 pounds yellow squash, sliced about
   ½-inch thick
2 teaspoons Cajun/Creole seasoning
2 teaspoons sugar

MELT 1 stick butter in a pot over medium-high to high heat. Sauté onion until tender. Add squash and Cajun/Creole seasoning. Add the remaining butter and sugar and cook over medium heat for 35 minutes.

SERVES 6 AS A SIDE DISH

Sweet Potato en Brochette

Wow, what a combination of flavors! This is an awesome way to impress your friends.

10 sweet potatoes, peeled
2 pounds sliced bacon
1 cup Steen's cane syrup (can substitute
   maple syrup or honey)

PREHEAT OVEN to 350 degrees.

SLICE EACH sweet potato lengthwise into four slices and wrap each slice in bacon. Place the sweet potatoes in a large baking pan and bake for 40 minutes. Let cool to just above room temperature and then drizzle with the syrup.

SERVES 10 AS A SIDE DISH

Bordelonville Corn and Ham Hock Soup

The corn grows quick in the sub-tropical weather of Cajun Country and the abundant supply of "mais tendre" corn facilitates a wide range of delicious recipes. Fresh corn from the cob works well in this recipe, so cut the corn from the cob and scrape its milk into a large bowl.

3 pounds fresh ham hocks (1-inch thick each)
3 teaspoons cooking oil
2 medium onions, chopped
1 large green bell pepper, chopped
1 stalk celery, chopped
3 teaspoons Cajun/Creole seasoning
2 cloves garlic, chopped
3 teaspoons flour
3¾ cups chicken broth or stock
4½ cups water
3 pounds fresh (with corn milk) or frozen whole kernel corn
2 (15-ounce) cans cream-style corn
Cornbread, optional

BROWN HAM hocks in oil on both sides until golden brown. Add onions, bell pepper, celery, and Cajun/Creole seasoning and sauté until the vegetables are tender.

ADD GARLIC and sauté for a few minutes, being careful not to burn. Add flour and stir until a blond roux forms, about 5 minutes. Deglaze slowly with the broth and water. Add the whole kernel corn and cream-style corn. Cook the soup for 1½ hours over medium heat. Serve in soup bowls with cornbread on the side, if desired.

SERVES 8

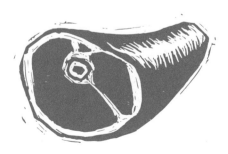

Pappa Breaux's Squirrel Supper

One of the greatest rites of passage in our family is turning 10 and going squirrel hunting with my dad. He takes the difficult hunt seriously and only bags his limit. Dad makes the best squirrel gravy in the world. On those cold and damp afternoons after the game is cleaned and consumed, we sit and talk of hunts to come.

8 cleaned squirrels (store-bought rabbit can be substituted), seasoned with Cajun/Creole seasoning
4 tablespoons cooking oil
1 (12-ounce) can amber beer
3 onions, chopped
3 green bell peppers, chopped
3 cloves garlic, chopped
1 (15-ounce) can chicken broth
1 (10.5-ounce) can French onion soup
1 tablespoon chicken base
3 teaspoons Cajun/Creole seasoning
4 cups cooked Louisiana rice

IN A large heavy pot, cook seasoned squirrels over high heat in oil until well browned. Remove the squirrels and deglaze pan with the beer. Sauté onions and bell peppers until limp. Add garlic and sauté 3 minutes more, being careful not to burn. Deglaze pan with the broth, then add the condensed soup, chicken base, and Cajun/Creole seasoning and stir well. Add the squirrels back to the pan to finish cooking. Cover and cook over medium heat for 1½ hours, stirring occasionally. Serve over ½ cup cooked rice per serving.

SERVES 8

Lebeau Okra Gumbo

Some of the best duck and goose hunting in Louisiana is in the rice fields of Lebeau. This gumbo satisfies the soul and enables a fellow to sleep in oblivion.

OKRA
¼ cup cooking oil
4 pounds okra, sliced ¼-inch thick
3 teaspoons white vinegar
1 (14-ounce) can stewed tomatoes
2 teaspoons Cajun/Creole seasoning

GUMBO
3 teaspoons cooking oil
Large whole fryer chicken, cut into
   8 pieces (about 4 pounds)
1 large onion, chopped
1 medium green bell pepper, chopped
1 teaspoon Cajun/Creole seasoning
1 clove garlic, chopped
4¼ cups chicken broth
3 cups water
¼ cup roux (see page 28)
1 bunch green onions, chopped
1 bunch parsley, chopped
4 cups cooked Louisiana rice

TO COOK the okra, add oil to a preheated heavy-gauge aluminum pot. Add okra, vinegar, tomatoes, and Cajun/Creole seasoning. Cook for 1 hour over medium heat, stirring often to prevent scorching. Turn off heat and let sit.

TO COOK the gumbo, add oil to a large soup pot and brown chicken pieces until golden brown. Add the onion, bell pepper, and Cajun/Creole seasoning to pot and sauté until vegetables are very tender. Add garlic and sauté for a couple of minutes. Deglaze with broth and add water, and then bring to a boil. Add roux and stir until completely dissolved. Cook for 30 minutes over medium heat. Add cooked okra and let cook for 30 minutes more. Turn off heat and add green onions and parsley. Serve in soup bowls over ½ cup cooked rice per serving.

SERVES 8

Marksville Goo with White Gravy

A friend of mine, Chris Villemarette, hails from Marksville, Louisiana. One day I was visiting with him at our family supermarket and noticed these ingredients in his shopping cart. Chris' eyes became focused as he described the way his grandma, Bessie Foster, fixes this dish. From his passionate expression I realized that I needed to try this wonderful meal. Thank God and Chris Villemarette for the revelation!

3 teaspoons cooking oil
1 medium baking hen, cut into
  serving-size pieces
2 medium onions, chopped
2 medium green bell peppers, chopped
1 stalk celery, chopped
2 cloves garlic, chopped
3 cups chicken broth or stock
1½ cups water
3 teaspoons Cajun/Creole seasoning
2 pounds fresh or frozen butter beans
1 bunch green onions, chopped
Cornbread, optional

HEAT OIL in a Dutch oven. Brown the hen in oil until golden brown. Remove from pot, add onions, bell peppers, and celery to the pot and sauté until very tender. Add garlic and sauté a few minutes more. Deglaze with broth and water. Return chicken to pot and add Cajun/Creole seasoning. Cover and cook for 1½ hours over medium heat. Add butter beans and cook, covered, for 30 minutes. Remove ½ cup of the beans and smash into a paste; stir back into pot and cook, uncovered, for 15 minutes more. Turn off heat and add green onions. Serve with slice of cornbread, if desired.

SERVES 10

Opelousas Catfish Gravy

Downtown Opelousas, Louisiana, resembles the architecture of New Orleans with wrought iron, historic churches, and a courthouse square. The area was home to the Spanish seat of government and later, the wealthy Creole French planters and commodity speculators. The cooks who accompanied the French from New Orleans and France introduced Creole tomato gravy.

¼ cup cooking oil
2 large onions, chopped
2 green bell peppers, chopped
1 stalk celery, chopped
2 mild banana peppers, seeded and chopped
1 (10-ounce) can chopped tomatoes with chiles
1 (8-ounce) can tomato sauce
1 cup fish stock
1 cup water
3 teaspoons Cajun/Creole seasoning
3 pounds catfish fillets
1 bunch green onions, chopped
1 bunch parsley, chopped
4 cups cooked Louisiana rice

ADD OIL to a medium-size Dutch oven. Add onions, bell peppers, celery, and banana peppers, and sauté until tender. Add tomatoes and sauté until thick and mixture starts to brown. Add tomato sauce, stock, water, and Cajun/Creole seasoning. Cook for 1½ hours over medium heat. Sauce will reduce by half. Add catfish fillets and cook for 25 minutes. Remove from heat and add green onions and parsley. Serve over ½ cup cooked rice per serving.

SERVES 8

Cottonport Jambalaya

Jambalaya is almost a religion in Louisiana. The northern part of Cajun Country incorporates pork and smoked sausage in their recipes, while other areas prefer chicken or seafood. Jambalaya is served at Cajun gatherings such as weddings, graduations, family reunions, tailgate parties, church socials, and charity golf tournaments.

¼ cup cooking oil
2 pounds boneless pork, cut into
   1-inch cubes
1 pound smoked sausage, cut into
   ½-inch slices
2 large onions, chopped
1 large green bell pepper, chopped
2 stalks celery, chopped
4 teaspoons Cajun/Creole seasoning
2 cloves garlic, chopped
1 (10.5-ounce) can French onion soup
2 cups beef broth
5 cups water
3 tablespoons roux (see page 28)
3 cups uncooked long-grain Louisiana rice
1 bunch green onions, chopped

ADD OIL to a hot large Dutch oven. Brown pork until golden brown. Add sausage, onions, bell pepper, celery, and Cajun/Creole seasoning, and sauté until vegetables are very tender and beginning to brown. Add garlic and sauté for a couple of minutes more. Do not burn garlic. Deglaze with condensed soup. Add broth and water, and bring to a boil. Add roux and stir to dissolve completely. Cover and cook over medium heat for 1 hour. Add rice and stir; cover tightly and cook for 25 minutes. Add green onions and stir. Cover and let sit 15 minutes and then serve.

SERVES 10

WILD ☞ ☜ GAME SERVED TO CAJUN PERFECTION

★ ★ ★

More so than any other region of Cajun Country, wild game has played an important role as the major protein source in the Upper Prairie Cajun diet. Skilled hunters and trappers perfected and honed their skills and methods of securing meat for their families.

Because of the large Catholic families, sauces and gravies were served over cornbread or rice in order to stretch the meal. The small country bars of South Louisiana are the unofficial campaign headquarters during an election year. Suppers are held and men gather to talk politics and eat great meals cooked by one of their buddies. Cajun men are very competitive when it comes to cooking; tons of praise is bestowed upon the most skilled cooks among us.

Old-Time Potatoes

Make sure that the couch or easy chair is near after consuming this hearty dish. A nap may be in order!

1 pound smoked sausage
3 tablespoons vegetable oil
½ cup chopped yellow onion
5 pounds red potatoes, quartered with
   skin on
2 teaspoons Cajun/Creole seasoning
2 cups chicken broth
3 cups water
1 bunch green onions, chopped

IN A Dutch oven, brown sausage. Add oil and sauté onion until translucent. Add the potatoes, Cajun/Creole seasoning, and broth and cook over medium heat, stirring to prevent sticking. As liquid evaporates, add water gradually, stirring frequently until potatoes are tender. Remove from heat; add green onions and stir.

SERVES 6

Green "Zydeco" Beans

The origins of zydeco music allegedly came from the song, "Les Haricots Sont Pas Salés," which literally means the green beans aren't salty, or the singer was too poor to put salt pork or bacon in his beans. Les Haricots (green beans) sounded like zydeco and the name stuck. These green beans are not only salty but also packed with layers of flavor.

½ pound sliced bacon
1 red bell pepper, chopped
¾ cup pearl onions
4 (15-ounce) cans French-style
    green beans
1 teaspoon Cajun/Creole seasoning

COOK BACON in a pot, then remove and crumble; leave 2 to 3 tablespoons bacon grease in the pot. Sauté bell pepper in the grease until tender, then add onions, cooked bacon, green beans, and Cajun/Creole seasoning. Cook over low heat for 20 minutes.

SERVES 12 AS A SIDE DISH

Cochon de Lait

The Cochon de Lait has its origins in northern Cajun Country in family and community celebrations. The men are the designated cooks of this delectable culinary treat as it is quite an endeavor to prepare. The event serves as a bonding opportunity for the community, as the young men observe the older men applying their long-practiced skill. Women prepare the side dishes for the meal, which includes sweet potatoes, rice dressing, and smothered cabbage.

1½ cups chopped onion
1 cup chopped green bell pepper
1 cup chopped celery
½ cup chopped garlic
½ cup white vinegar
1 cup Cajun/Creole seasoning, divided
1 whole suckling pig (40 pounds dressed)
Cajun Microwave*

MIX TOGETHER the onion, bell pepper, celery, garlic, vinegar, and ¼ cup Cajun/Creole seasoning. Cut many slits in the pig and stuff with the seasoned vegetable blend. Season entire outside of pig with the remaining seasoning. Place in a 350- to 400-degree Cajun Microwave, rib side up, and close. Cook for 3 hours. Turn pig over so that the skin faces the heat and cook for 2 hours more. Close and cover quickly to maintain temperature. Raise hog until it is only a few inches from the heat source. Score back in 2-inch squares. Close quickly in order to maintain temperature. Allow to cook for 30 minutes to crisp skin. Remove from Cajun Microwave and place on table whole. Let people serve themselves or set up a buffet line.

*CAJUN MICROWAVES can be used anywhere. They operate on charcoal much like a barbecue pit. To purchase or view a Cajun Microwave, visit www.cajunmicrowaves.com or other dealers online.

SERVES 25

Poché Bridge Venison Hind Quarter

On the corner of Highway 31 and Declouet Road in rural St. Martin Parish sits my favorite watering hole, Boy's Lounge. The patrons of this bar converse in Cajun French. This tends to startle the outsiders who are fortunate enough to find this living remnant of our cultural past. I stop at Boy's Lounge on hot summer afternoons after catching pan fish in the Atchafalaya Basin. I get to brag about my take of fish and quench my parched throat with ice cold beer. I cooked this recipe one fine spring day on the back porch of the lounge for fellow Francophone friends of mine.

¾ cup chopped onion
½ cup chopped green bell pepper
½ cup chopped celery
4 tablespoons chopped garlic
2 tablespoons white vinegar
6 tablespoons Cajun/Creole seasoning, divided
12 to 15 pounds venison hind, quartered (or substitute beef or pork roast)
2 bottles (750 mL each) blackberry wine
3 cups chicken broth
2 (16-ounce) jars salsa
2 (5-ounce) jars pearl onions
6 pears, cored
6 cups cooked Louisiana rice

MIX TOGETHER the first five ingredients and 2 tablespoons Cajun/Creole seasoning. Cut slits in roast and liberally stuff the mixture inside. Season outside of roast with the remaining seasoning. Grill the roast on all sides in order to seal the juices in. Place roast in a aluminum pan. Add wine, broth, salsa, and onions, and cover with foil. Cook over hot coals for 3½ hours. Add pears, cover, and cook 30 to 40 minutes more. Serve over ½ cup cooked rice per serving.

SERVES 12

CHAPTER 4: LOWER PRAIRIE

The Lower Prairie region of southwest Louisiana experienced similar Acadian settlement patterns as its northern counterpart did, with many of its residents appearing around 1766 and establishing towns during the following decades. By the nineteenth century, Cajuns would venture farther west toward the Texas border. The city of Lafayette developed as the center of this region, now referred to as "Acadiana," and its low unemployment, oil and gas industry, and hub of medical facilities keep it growing every year. Because of the strong Cajun culture and history, Lafayette is home to numerous outstanding Cajun restaurants. The "Hub City" is also home to two attractions that represent Cajun culture of another time: Acadian Village, a folklife museum, and Vermilionville, a living history attraction. Both contain a collection of authentic Cajun homes, buildings, schools, and churches consolidated into each location.

Hebert's Specialty Meats creates a unique twist for Thanksgiving— the turducken, a deboned turkey stuffed with a boneless duck and chicken with cornbread dressing and pork stuffing separating each poultry. Although it's debatable who started the sensation first, Paul Prudhomme or the Heberts, the Maurice meat market sells about 3,300 turduckens a year...

The Acadian Cultural Center of the Jean Lafitte National Historical Park and Preserve focuses on the history, customs, language, and contemporary culture of Louisiana's Cajuns, and the University of Louisiana at Lafayette offers a cypress swamp in the middle of its campus.

Lafayette is also home to the largest outdoor Francophone festival in the United States, International Festival de Louisiane, and the annual Festivals Acadiens et Creoles. Both offer many opportunities to dance to live Cajun music, and if you miss the annual fêtes, venues throughout Lafayette will provide plenty of opportunities.

In nearby Vermilion Parish, in the quaint town of Maurice, Hebert's Specialty Meats creates a unique twist for Thanksgiving— the turducken, a deboned turkey stuffed with a boneless duck and chicken with cornbread dressing and pork stuffing separating each poultry. Although it's debatable who started the sensation first, Paul Prudhomme or the Heberts, the Maurice meat market sells about 3,300 turduckens a year and was spotlighted in *National Geographic*.

Abbeville is the parish seat of Vermilion Parish, a town created by Father Antoine Jacques Désiré Mégret of Abbeville, France. Every year, Abbeville celebrates its French heritage with the Giant Omelete Festival. Several restaurants specialize in oysters brought in from the bays and Gulf and local agriculture includes rice, crawfish, alligators, and cattle.

Down the road in a converted bank building you'll find the

Acadian Museum of Erath, providing the entire history of the Acadians, from France to Louisiana, in addition to the town's history. Warren A. Perrin, museum founder and president of the Council for the Development of French in Louisiana, petitioned Queen Elizabeth II for an apology for the Acadian deportation and received an official reply in 2003. The "Queen's Proclamation" is proudly displayed in the museum today.

The many murals in downtown Rayne depict why it is titled the "Frog Capital of the World." At the turn of the twentieth century, the town farmed bullfrogs for the country's restaurants, including fine dining establishments in New York City. Rayne celebrates its amphibious heritage with the annual Rayne Frog Festival in early September, and Chef Roy's Frog City Café offers fried frog legs and frog étouffée on the menu—as well as gumbo, crawfish, shrimp, and crab cakes.

About two hundred homes and buildings are on the National Register of Historic Places in Crowley, but the prairie town is best known for its annual International Rice Festival where one lucky cook receives the honor of Chef de Riz, or grand-prize winner of the Rice Creole and Cookery Contest sponsored by the Louisiana State University AgCenter.

And don't miss stopping at Suire's Grocery in Kaplan for some crawfish pistolettes and boudin.

Locally produced food products of the Lower Prairie include Falcon Rice of Crowley, Steen's one hundred percent cane syrup and Cajun Power sauces from Abbeville, and Mello Joy coffee in Lafayette.

Vermilionville Chicken Fricassee

Chicken fricassee is a dish that most exemplifies Cajun comfort food. Many fond memories and food cravings are associated with this dish—it's pretty darn good!

1 fryer chicken, cut into
   serving-size pieces
2 tablespoons cooking oil
3 teaspoons Cajun/Creole seasoning,
   divided
¾ cup chopped onion, divided
½ cup chopped green bell pepper, divided
½ cup chopped celery, divided
4 tablespoons chopped garlic, divided
3 cups chicken broth or stock, divided
2 cups water
3 tablespoons chicken base
½ cup roux (see page 28)
4 cups cooked Louisiana rice

BROWN CHICKEN pieces in oil over medium-high heat for 12 minutes in a medium soup pot. Season chicken with 1 teaspoon Cajun/Creole seasoning and remove from pot. Add half of the onion, bell pepper, celery, and garlic to pot and sauté for 5 to 7 minutes until limp. Deglaze with ¾ cup broth. Add the rest of broth, water, chicken base, and remaining vegetables. Add roux and stir until completely dissolved. Return chicken to pot. Add the remaining Cajun/Creole seasoning and cook over medium heat for 45 minutes. Serve over ½ cup cooked rice per serving.

SERVES 8

Henry Smothered Rabbit and Fresh Sausage

Rabbit hunting is serious business to the Cajuns of South Louisiana. When I was a child I knew a man named Paul Alfred who would hunt rabbits with a stick. He would sneak up on them in the dead of winter and strike at their heads, taking them in one blow. Paul Alfred had 22 children, a lot of mouths to feed, and hunting was an important part of their food supply. This recipe is one of the favorite ways it is prepared in Cajun country.

2 to 3 pounds domestic rabbits, cut into
    serving-size pieces
4 tablespoons cooking oil
2 pounds fresh pork sausage
2 medium onions, chopped
1 medium green bell pepper, chopped
1 stalk celery, chopped
2 cloves garlic, chopped
1 (15-ounce) can chicken broth
3 cups water
3 teaspoons Cajun/Creole seasoning
1 bunch green onions, chopped
4 cups cooked Louisiana rice

BROWN RABBIT pieces in oil in a Dutch oven over medium-high heat until golden brown. Remove meat and set aside. Brown sausage whole in the same pot until firm and golden brown on all sides. Remove sausage, cut into bite-size pieces and set aside. Add the onions, bell pepper, and celery to the pot and sauté until very tender and browning starts. Add garlic and sauté for 3 minutes. Deglaze pot with broth. Return the rabbit and sausage to the pot and add the water and Cajun/Creole seasoning. Cook partially covered over medium heat for 1½ hours. Remove from heat. Add green onions and serve on a plate over ½ cup cooked rice per serving.

SERVES 8

Avery Island Shrimp Gumbo

I cooked this shrimp gumbo on a shrimp boat at the Delcambre, Louisiana, Christmas Parade. The celebration is held next to the docks along the bayou and the parade rolls at sunset on the waterway. The boats are lit up with Christmas lights and pass by as fireworks explode in the winter sky.

8 cups shrimp or seafood stock
8 cups water
2 cups roux (page 28)
2 medium onions, chopped
1 medium green bell pepper, chopped
1 rib celery, chopped
3 ounces dry shrimp powder (available in Asian grocery stores)
5 teaspoons Cajun/Creole seasoning
3 pounds medium shrimp, cleaned and deveined
1 bunch green onions, chopped
1 bunch parsley, chopped
5 cups cooked Louisiana rice

BRING THE shrimp stock and water to a boil in a large soup pot. Add the roux and stir until completely dissolved. Add the onions, bell pepper, celery, shrimp powder, and Cajun/Creole seasoning and cook over medium-high heat for 45 minutes. Gumbo will reduce. Add shrimp and cook over medium heat for 20 minutes. Remove from heat. Add the green onions and parsley. Let sit for 30 minutes and serve in soup bowls over 1/2 cup cooked rice per serving.

SERVES 10

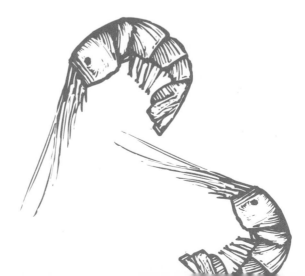

Turtle Soup Bayou Queue de Tortue

South Louisiana has an incredible population of various species of turtles. My personal favorite is the yellow belly variety as it cooks tender and the meat has a sweet taste. As a child I remember an old man named Fabous who used to catch them in the rice canals by my grandpa's farm.

4 pounds turtle meat
4 tablespoons cooking oil
2 medium onions, chopped
2 medium green bell peppers, chopped
2 stalks celery, chopped
1 (10-ounce) can Rotel tomatoes
3 cloves garlic, chopped
5¾ cups beef broth or stock
3 cups water
⅓ cup dark roux (see page 28)
2 tablespoons beef base
3 bay leaves
¼ teaspoon nutmeg
¼ teaspoon rosemary
1 teaspoon thyme
3 teaspoons Cajun/Creole seasoning
3 teaspoons Worcestershire sauce
¼ cup dry sherry
1 bunch green onions, chopped
1 bunch parsley, chopped
5 hard-boiled eggs, chopped
1 loaf French bread

BROWN TURTLE meat in oil in a large Dutch oven until well browned on all sides. Add onions, bell peppers, celery, and tomatoes, and sauté until tender. Add garlic and sauté for a few minutes more. Deglaze with broth and water. Bring liquid to a boil and then add roux and beef base; stir to dissolve. Add bay leaves, nutmeg, rosemary, thyme, Cajun/Creole seasoning, and Worcestershire sauce. Cook over medium heat for 2 hours. Sauce will reduce by half. Add dry sherry and cook for 20 to 25 minutes to remove alcohol. Remove from heat and add green onions, parsley, and eggs. Serve in soup bowls with crusty French bread for dipping.

SERVES 12

Pine Leaf Boys White Beans

The Pine Leaf Boys are Cajun musicians dedicated to preserving our world-renowned music. I cooked this at the Blue Moon Saloon in Lafayette, Louisiana, and thought it was the least I could do to honor such a fantastic group of musicians and friends.

1 pound tasso, diced
1 pound smoked sausage, cut into
 ½-inch slices
2 tablespoons olive oil
¾ cup chopped onion
½ cup chopped bell pepper
½ cup chopped celery
4 tablespoons chopped garlic
1 teaspoon Cajun/Creole seasoning
1 (15-ounce) can chicken broth
3 (28-ounce) cans white beans
4 cups cooked Louisiana rice

SAUTÉ TASSO and sausage in oil until brown. Add vegetables and Cajun/Creole seasoning, and sauté until vegetables are tender. Add chicken broth and beans. Cook over medium heat for 35 to 40 minutes, or until reduced and thick. Serve over ½ cup cooked rice per serving.

SERVES 8

Grandpa Howard's Crawfish Rice

The good thing about rice fields is that they are perfect habitats for crawfish. If they go well together in the field, they would probably be good together in a recipe, right?

1 pound Louisiana crawfish
1 (14-ounce) can quartered artichoke
 hearts, reserving ½ of the liquid in can
1 stick butter, cut into large pieces
4 cups cooked Louisiana rice
1½ teaspoons Cajun/Creole seasoning
1 bunch green onions, chopped

MIX ALL ingredients together. Place in a foil bag or pan and place on pit for 20 to 25 minutes, turning or stirring several times. Cover or seal tightly to allow to steam.

SERVES 4

Catahoula Catfish Courtbouillon

The tomato gravy with just a hint of roux is easier on the stomach in the summer heat of South Louisiana.

2 medium onions, chopped
1 large green bell pepper, chopped
1 stalk celery, chopped
2 tablespoons cooking oil
1 (4-ounce) can tomato paste
2 cloves garlic, chopped
1 (12-ounce) can Rotel tomatoes
2 bay leaves
4¼ cups seafood stock
1 (12-ounce) can V8 tomato juice
3 teaspoons Cajun/Creole seasoning
½ cup roux (see page 28)
3 pounds catfish fillets
Cooked Louisiana rice, optional
French bread, optional

SAUTÉ THE onions, bell pepper, and celery in oil over medium heat until soft in a Dutch oven. Add the tomato paste and brown. Add garlic, tomatoes, and bay leaves, and cook down until it slightly begins to brown. Add seafood stock, V8 juice, and Cajun/Creole seasoning. Bring to a boil. Add roux and stir until completely dissolved. Cook over medium-low heat for 1 hour. Add catfish fillets and cook for 25 minutes. Do not stir too much as the fish will break into small pieces. Serve over cooked rice or as a soup with French bread, if desired.

SERVES 10

Frog Sauce Piquante

The Cajun French word for bullfrog is *ouaouaron*, pronounced "waa-waa-ron" because of the sound they make on those dark nights in the swamp. We did not have frogs like these in Nova Scotia so therefore had no word for them. We adopted the word from our Attakapas Indian friends who showed us how to harvest them.

2 (4-ounce) cans tomato paste
¾ cup chopped onion
½ cup chopped green bell pepper
½ cup chopped celery
4 tablespoons chopped garlic
1 medium green bell pepper, julienned
1 medium onion, julienned
3 (15-ounce) cans tomato sauce
4¼ cups chicken broth
3 tablespoons chicken base
1 tablespoon fish bouillon
3 teaspoons Cajun/Creole seasoning
2 (10-ounce) cans Rotel tomatoes
8 to 10 whole frogs, cleaned
½ bunch parsley, finely chopped
5 cups cooked Louisiana rice

IN A large pot, brown the tomato paste until a rusty brown color. Add the vegetables and sauté for 8 to 10 minutes over medium-high heat. Add the tomato sauce, broth, chicken base, fish bouillon, Cajun/Creole seasoning, and tomatoes, and cook over medium heat for 3 hours. Add frogs and cook for 12 to 15 minutes. Remove from heat and add parsley. Serve over ½ cup cooked rice per serving.

SERVES 10

BAYOU
COURTABLEAU

★ ★ ★

Bayou Courtableau is isolated from the twenty-first century because of its geographic location, surrounded by thickly overgrown swamp to the north and west, and the formidable Atchafalaya Basin to the south and east. The great flood of 1927 was a catastrophe of biblical proportions. The complete and utter failure of the levee system allowed billions of gallons of raging water to inundate a fourth of the state of Louisiana, drowning many poor souls. Untold amounts of livestock perished and hundreds of thousands of acres of farmland were devastated. In an effort to alleviate the possibility of such a calamity recurring, the Army Corps of Engineers developed the massive levee and lock system to contain the Atchafalaya and Mississippi rivers.

It is truly amazing to see the levee control system at work, all the way from Ohio to the Gulf of Mexico. I remember the flood in the spring of 1973. As a young boy it was fascinating to see white tail deer in Acadiana Park, located in the beautiful rolling hills of northern Lafayette. The rising waters forced many wild animals from the Atchafalaya Basin to seek shelter on higher ground. That spring, Mother Nature almost won her battle to change the course of the Mississippi River. The Old River control structure was almost undermined as the water formed a giant whirlpool and began to tunnel under the locks. If not for the Army Corps of Engineers' untiring efforts, the tragedy of 1927 would have been repeated. Nature has a way of putting everything in perspective.

As a child, I would venture to the levee with my father and family for fishing trips, crawfish boils, barbecues, and hunting expeditions. Master Breaux (Mac), my grandfather, had a camp located on the Bayou Amy side of the levee. There my mom, Lillian Landry Breaux, would sit in an old chair in the shade and fish from the bank of the bayou for hours. An occasional shriek of joy would indicate that she had caught yet another fish.

There is a certain generational tie that occurs in families who fish or hunt together that overrides gender or age. I fish with my daughter, Madeleine (Catain), with hopes that one day when I am old and broken down she will reciprocate and bring me to cast my rod and share quiet moments.

I now venture to the levee as often as possible. The feel of gravel beneath your tires is intoxicating as your truck glides upon a cloud of dust on a hot summer day or slips and slides on a wet winter day. Often my destination is a camp on the Courtableau where life is simple and time moves slowly.

Fried Frogs

The tremendous amounts of bayous, swamps, marshes, and rice fields in South Louisiana provide an unbelievable harvest of frogs. This recipe is one of my favorite ways to serve these delectable culinary treats.

10 whole frogs, cleaned
3 teaspoons Cajun/Creole seasoning, divided
2 cups milk
4 eggs
4 cups flour
Frying-grade olive oil
1 cantaloupe, sliced

SEASON FROGS with 1 teaspoon Cajun/Creole seasoning. Mix the milk, eggs, and 1 teaspoon Cajun/Creole seasoning in a bowl. Place the frogs in mixture and let sit for 15 minutes. Dredge frogs in a mixture of flour and 1 teaspoon Cajun/Creole seasoning, then pan-fry at 350 degrees in oil for 3 minutes on each side. Serve with sliced cantaloupe.

SERVES 5

Cajun Style Brisket

The Acadians are French descendants and as a result still retain a lot of European traditions and customs, such as a more relaxed lifestyle. Daylong celebrations such as birthdays, Catholic confirmations, anniversaries, and festivals are commonplace. This recipe allows for hours of merriment before the meal is served.

3 tablespoons Cajun/Creole seasoning
10- to 12-pound brisket (do not trim fat)

BRISKET GRAVY
1 medium onion, julienned
3 tablespoons butter
1¼ cups beef broth
Brisket drippings
1½ tablespoons beef base
2 tablespoons flour
1 cup water

PREHEAT OVEN to 425 degrees.

RUB CAJUN/CREOLE seasoning on brisket, coating well. Place in a large baking aluminum pan and cover tightly with foil. Bake for 4 hours, fat side up. Brisket fat will scrape off like butter. Save fat and make into gravy.

TO MAKE the gravy, place the onion and butter in a covered dish in the microwave for 3 minutes on high, then place in a saucepan with broth and brisket drippings (with fat skimmed off) and heat until boiling. Dissolve the beef base in the gravy.

IN A separate container, dissolve the flour in water and pour into boiling gravy, whisking constantly until desired thickness.

SERVES 10

Corn Macque Choux—Chitimacha Nation

The indigenous people of Louisiana influenced many of the dishes we consume. This dish combines the ingredients that were available to the Chitimacha tribal people.

6 ears fresh corn on the cob
2 medium yellow onions, chopped
1 large green bell pepper, chopped
3 stalks celery, chopped
2 sticks butter, divided
3 tablespoons olive oil
1 (12-ounce) can chopped tomatoes
  with chiles
3 cloves garlic, chopped
1 (15-ounce) can cream-style corn
1½ cups chicken broth
2 tablespoons Cajun/Creole seasoning
1 pound Louisiana crawfish tail meat
4 cups cooked Louisiana rice

SCRAPE THE corn off the cob into a bowl and set aside, making sure to harvest the milk as well. Sauté the onions, bell pepper, and celery in 1 stick of butter and the oil until tender. Add the tomatoes and garlic and sauté for 5 to 7 minutes. Add cream-style corn and broth and season with Cajun/Creole seasoning. Add crawfish and remaining butter and cook over medium heat for 20 minutes. Serve over ½ cup cooked rice per serving.

SERVES 8

Louisiana Rice Harvest Brown Gravy

The flat prairie land of this region of Acadiana is perfect for raising cattle. Beef, rice, and gravy rules.

3 tablespoons cooking oil
3 pounds chuck or shoulder steak
2½ teaspoons Cajun/Creole seasoning
1¼ cups chopped onion
¾ cup chopped green bell pepper
¾ cup chopped celery
4 tablespoons chopped garlic
1 cup beer
1 tablespoon beef base
3 cups water
1 bunch green onions, chopped
4 cups cooked Louisiana rice

ADD OIL to a hot Dutch oven and place steak in pot, browning over medium-high heat for 35 minutes, turning frequently. Season with Cajun/Creole seasoning in several steps. Remove meat and add vegetables; sauté until soft and some browning occurs. Deglaze bottom of pot with beer and scrape to dissolve the residue. Dissolve the beef base in the pot and return the meat. Add enough water to cover the meat, then cover pot and cook over medium heat for 1½ hours, adding water as needed. When gravy is thick enough to coat spoon, turn off heat and add green onions. Serve over ½ cup cooked rice per serving.

SERVES 8

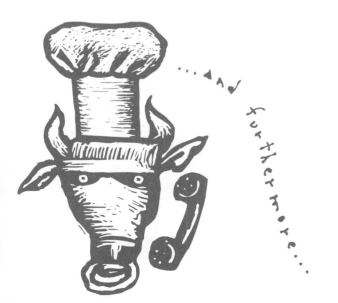

...and furthermore...

Rabbit Island Duck Gumbo

Wild ducks have little body fat left on them when they reach the end of their journey south for the winter migration. The introduction of the fresh pork sausage to this gumbo provides loads of flavor and a richness that makes a Cajun man proud to share with friends at the camp. Teal and wood duck are famous for their delicious meat.

6 teal or wood duck, quartered
4 teaspoons Cajun/Creole seasoning, divided
1 tablespoon cooking oil
2 pounds fresh pork sausage
1 (15-ounce) can duck or chicken stock
1 gallon water
1 cup dark roux (see page 28)
3 medium onions, chopped
1 large green bell pepper, chopped
1 stalk celery, chopped
1 bunch green onion, chopped
1 bunch parsley, chopped
6 cups cooked Louisiana rice

SEASON THE quartered ducks with 2 teaspoons Cajun/Creole seasoning. Brown the ducks in oil in a medium soup pot over medium-high heat for 25 minutes, turning often. Remove and set aside. Put whole fresh sausage in pot and brown. Remove and set aside. Deglaze the pot with stock. Add water and bring to a boil. Add roux and stir until completely dissolved. Add onions, bell pepper, celery, and the remaining Cajun/Creole seasoning. Return duck and sausage to pot. Let cook for 20 minutes, then remove sausage and cut into bite-size pieces before returning to pot. Cook over medium heat until meat starts to separate from the bone. Turn off heat and add green onions and parsley. Let sit for 15 minutes. Serve over 1/2 cup cooked rice per serving.

SERVES 12

Carencro Ranch Style Beans

Cattle ranches dot the countryside in Louisiana due to mild winters and the availability of pastureland. The trail rides are an important part of social gatherings. At the end of a ride, bands perform, dancing starts, and massive quantities of food are consumed.

1 pound sliced bacon
½ cup chopped onion
¼ cup chopped green bell pepper
¼ cup chopped celery
2 tablespoons chopped garlic
5 (15-ounce) cans ranch-style beans
2 tablespoons chicken base
½ cup honey
1 teaspoon Cajun/Creole seasoning

IN A Dutch oven over medium heat, cook bacon until crisp. Remove from pot, crumble, and set aside. Add vegetables to bacon grease and sauté over medium heat until limp. Add beans, chicken base, honey, crumbled bacon, and Cajun/Creole seasoning. Cook over low heat for 30 minutes.

SERVES 10

Abbeville Syrup Cake

Abbeville is home to Steen's Cane Syrup, which we always use in this cake.

1 cup light brown sugar
1 cup cane syrup (preferably Steen's)
2 cups flour
½ cup oil
2 eggs
1½ teaspoons baking powder
½ teaspoon vanilla
½ teaspoon nutmeg
½ teaspoon cinnamon
½ cup boiling water
Whipped cream (optional)

PREHEAT OVEN to 350 degrees.

MIX TOGETHER all ingredients except water and whipped cream. Add the boiling water and mix well. Pour into a 9 x 13-inch greased pan and bake for 35 minutes. Top with whipped cream.

SERVES 12

VARIATION: ADD ½ cup raisins.

CHAPTER 5
★ ★ ★
THE BAYOU REGION

The largest group of Acadians to enter Louisiana was those repatriated to France following their exile from Nova Scotia. In France, this group fought off attempts by the French government to absorb them into society. They petitioned Spain to allow them to travel to Louisiana, which was under Spanish rule, and become independent farmers once again. They were granted entrance in 1785, arriving near the town of St. Martinville. Today, the Acadian Memorial in St. Martinville honors the history of the Cajun people and their plight with a massive mural by Lafayette artist Robert Dafford depicting those fifteen hundred souls who stepped off the boats and into a new world. Many people will remember St. Martinville from the poem *Evangeline* by Henry Wadsworth Longfellow. It was the first published account of the Acadian deportation and brought nationwide

Around Mardi Gras, St. Martinville continues the tradition of *La Grande Boucherie des Cajuns,* or communal hog butchering where cracklins are cooked and fresh pork is served. New Iberia, home to Tabasco at nearby Avery Island, hosts an annual hot sauce festival in the spring and the popular Sugarcane Festival in the fall.

attention to a people who were silently thrown from their land. Thousands of people visit the "Evangeline Oak" on the banks of Bayou Teche each year and nearby is the Longfellow-Evangeline State Historic Site with its living example of early-eighteenth-century architecture.

The Bayou Region is home to culturally rich historic towns and numerous scenic bayous and wetlands. Breaux Bridge boasts of being the "crawfish capital of the world" and celebrates the state crustacean every May with the Breaux Bridge Crawfish Festival. Around Mardi Gras, St. Martinville continues the tradition of *La Grande Boucherie des Cajuns,* or communal hog butchering where cracklins are cooked and fresh pork is served. New Iberia, home to Tabasco at nearby Avery Island, hosts an annual hot sauce festival in the spring and the popular Sugarcane Festival in the fall. Arnaudville, once known as "La Jonction" because of its position at the confluence of Bayou Teche and Bayou Fuselier, hosts an annual Étouffée Festival that honors the tradition of smothered dishes from crawfish to chicken.

And the town of Henderson exists along the levee of the Atchafalaya Basin, the largest river drainage swamp in

North America. Here, visitors can enjoy great seafood from the Basin, fish in its abundant waters, and take swamp tours led by Cajuns who have spent their lives within its majestic wetlands.

In New Iberia, America's oldest rice mill shares its history with tourists at the Konriko Company Store. Built in 1912 by founder Phillip Conrad Sr., visitors can watch workers package rice and make rice cakes. At Avery Island, tourists can witness Tabasco being bottled and learn of its long, hot history, in addition to touring the gardens and egret rookery. Bruce Foods is located in New Iberia as well, producing Cajun and Tex Mex products for more than 80 years, including Louisiana brand hot pepper sauce and Cajun Injector products.

Jeanerette is located among acres and acres of sugarcane fields, so it's no wonder the Jeanerette Museum features exhibits on the long history of sugar cane growing in Louisiana. LeJeune's Bakery in Jeanerette continues its long family tradition and sells some of the finest French bread in Acadiana.

Old-Time Catfish and Crawfish Sauce Piquante

The town Port Barre was an important trading community of the early 1700s. Bayou Courtableau and Bayou Fusilier served as highways to transport goods and crops from New Orleans to a large part of South Louisiana. The bayous provided the crawfish and catfish so crucial to this recipe.

3 tablespoons tomato paste
2 tablespoons cooking oil
2 medium onions, chopped
2 medium green bell peppers, chopped
½ stalk celery, chopped
1 (10-ounce) can diced tomatoes
  with chiles
4½ cups water
2 tablespoons roux (see page 28)
4 cloves garlic, chopped
1 seafood bouillon cube
1 (4-ounce) can tomato sauce
2 teaspoons Cajun/Creole seasoning
2 pounds catfish fillets
1 pound peeled Louisiana crawfish tails
4 cups cooked Louisiana rice

IN A heavy pot, brown the tomato paste until rusty in color. Add oil and sauté onions, bell peppers, celery, and tomatoes until tender. Add water to deglaze, then dissolve roux into mixture and add garlic and seafood bouillon. Add tomato sauce and Cajun/Creole seasoning. Cook for 1 hour, adding water as needed. Add catfish and crawfish and cook for 15 to 20 minutes. Serve over ½ cup cooked rice per serving.

SERVES 8

Lake Pelba Black-Eyed Peas

The gardens of the Atchafalaya Basin were restricted by the seasonal flooding that occurred yearly. Fresh produce was grown at practically every home; the vegetables were mostly consumed as they ripened on the stalk or vine. The Basin Cajuns traded for supplies such as potatoes and dried beans that could be stored and cooked with smoked meat. Black-eyed peas cooked this way can be served over cooked rice as a full meal.

1 pound pork tasso
1 tablespoon cooking oil
½ cup chopped onions
¼ cup chopped bell pepper
¼ cup chopped celery
2 tablespoons chopped garlic
1 (15-ounce) can chicken broth
2 pounds fresh or frozen black-eyed peas
1 tablespoon chicken base
2 teaspoons Cajun/Creole seasoning

LIGHTLY BROWN tasso in oil, then add the onion, bell pepper, celery, and garlic, and sauté until limp. Deglaze with chicken broth. Add black-eyed peas, chicken base, and Cajun/Creole seasoning, and cook over medium heat for 40 minutes.

SERVES 6

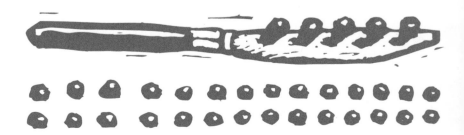

Okra St. Martin

Smothered okra often is a main dish on the dinner tables of South Louisiana. The addition of chicken and shrimp to this recipe, served over rice with potato salad on the side, makes a delightful Sunday meal.

1 pound smoked sausage, cut into
  1-inch slices
3 tablespoons cooking oil
1 (15-ounce) can tomatoes with chiles
3 pounds cut okra, cut into
  ½-inch-thick slices
1½ teaspoons Cajun/Creole seasoning
1 cup water
1 tablespoon white vinegar

BROWN SAUSAGE in oil over medium heat. Add tomatoes and brown slightly. Add okra and Cajun/Creole seasoning and stir well to coat with oil. Add water and vinegar. Cover and cook over medium heat for 35 to 40 minutes.

SERVES 4

Bayou Teche Garfish Balls

The addition of catfish to this recipe adds a wonderful texture to these golden treats.

1 pound garfish, ground
1 pound catfish, ground
1 cup saltine cracker crumbs
2 eggs, beaten
1½ teaspoons Cajun/Creole seasoning
Cooking oil for frying

IN A mixing bowl, combine the garfish, catfish, cracker crumbs, eggs, and Cajun/Creole seasoning. Form into balls about the size of a golf ball. Deep-fry in 350-degree oil until golden brown.

SERVES 6

Sac-A-Lait at Cypress Cove Landing

In the heat of late June, the sac-a-lait fishing begins to peak in the Atchafalaya Basin. The flesh of this fish is treasured by aquatic meat aficionados.

2 cups milk
1 cup mustard
4 eggs
2 teaspoons red hot sauce
2 teaspoons green hot sauce
2 teaspoons Cajun/Creole seasoning
12 sac-a-lait (crappie) fish fillets
32 ounces Louisiana Fish Fry (seasoned cornmeal)
1 gallon peanut oil

MIX FIRST six ingredients together. Place room temperature fish in mixture and let sit for 20 minutes. Pour fish fry into a gallon-size plastic bag. Place fish, a couple at a time, in the bag and shake until coated. Fry fish in oil at 350 degrees for 6 to 7 minutes per batch.

SERVES 6

St. Martin Alligator Eggs

These little jewels are great for appetizers at holiday parties or tailgating events. I fix them for my friends at the duck camp on just about every hunting trip.

10 jalepeños, halved and seeded
¼ pound ground smoked sausage
¼ pound ground tasso
⅓ pound sharp cheddar cheese, grated
1 pound sliced bacon
Vegetable oil for frying

CHILL JALEPEÑOS in freezer for 30 minutes. Combine sausage, tasso, and cheese. Stuff the halved and seeded peppers with the mixture. Wrap with bacon and cut off excess if needed. Spear bacon-wrapped jalepeños with toothpicks. Fry in 350-degree oil for about 4 to 5 minutes.

SERVES 5

Breaux Bridge Garfish Roast

The rice canals of Cajun Country provide a source of water to the agricultural communities as well as recreational opportunities for swimmers and anglers alike. Garfish look like prehistoric creatures from a science fiction movie. The flesh of the garfish is much like swordfish or shark and can be browned like a pork roast. This a favorite freshwater fish recipe.

4 pounds garfish roast, cut into
   large chunks
3 tablespoons olive oil
1 cup water
2 onions, chopped
2 green bell peppers, chopped
4 cloves garlic, chopped
2 stalks celery, chopped
2½ teaspoons Cajun/Creole seasoning,
   divided
1 (12-ounce) can diced tomatoes
   with peppers
2 cups seafood stock
¼ cup chopped green onions
¼ cup chopped parsley
6 cups cooked Louisiana rice

PREHEAT THE oven to 350 degrees.

BROWN GARFISH in a heavy pot in oil until well browned on all sides. Remove from pot and deglaze with water. Add the vegetables to the pot and season with 1 teaspoon Cajun/Creole seasoning. Sauté until soft and starting to brown. Add tomatoes and sauté until the mixture starts to brown. Add stock to deglaze and add the remaining seasoning. Return garfish to pot and cover. Bake for 1½ hours. Remove and stir in green onions and parsley. Serve over cooked rice.

SERVES 10

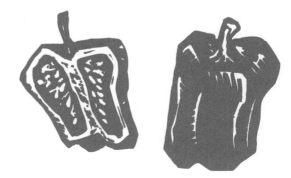

Evangeline Oak Shrimp and Oyster en Brochettes

This is a recipe that I cooked under the Evangeline Oak in St. Martinville, Louisiana. I was breaking down equipment after shooting an episode of my TV cooking show and cleaning up the area. I returned to find that the crew and spectators had eaten every single one of these jewels.

1 pound medium Louisiana shrimp,
　peeled and deveined
1 pint Louisiana oysters
1 pound sliced bacon
1 teaspoon Cajun/Creole seasoning
Vegetable oil for frying
16 ounces pepper jack cheese, grated

PLACE 1 shrimp and 1 oyster on a slice of bacon and roll up. Cut excess bacon if needed. Spear with toothpick. Repeat steps for the whole batch. Dust with Cajun/Creole seasoning and fry in 350-degree oil for about 5 minutes. Remove from oil and dust with more Cajun/Creole seasoning. Top with cheese.

SERVES 6

Acadian Memorial Jambalaya

The Acadian people of Louisiana suffered immensely as a result of the expulsion from Canada. Families were purposely separated in an almost successful attempt at genocide. The eventual generosity of the Spanish crown enabled the survivors to locate in Louisiana and the importance of preserving family has prevailed. The Cajuns of Louisiana often have family gatherings with extended families. Third cousins are considered close relations in this part of the U.S. This recipe provided an inexpensive way to serve all of these cousins.

3 pounds fresh sausage
2 tablespoons olive oil
5 pounds boneless chicken thighs, cut into bite-size pieces
¾ cup chopped onion
½ cup chopped green bell pepper
½ cup chopped celery
4 tablespoons chopped garlic
4 cups chicken broth or stock
3 tablespoons chicken base
3 cups water
3 teaspoons Cajun/Creole seasoning
10 cups cooked Louisiana rice
1 bunch green onions, chopped

BROWN SAUSAGE in oil for 7 minutes, then add chicken and brown for 10 minutes over high heat. Add vegetables, stir to deglaze and cook for 5 minutes, stirring frequently. Add stock, chicken base, water, and Cajun/Creole seasoning. Cook for 45 minutes over medium heat, Add cooked rice and green onions. Stir well and serve.

SERVES 24

ALL ABOUT LOUISIANA CRAWFISH

★ ★ ★

Crawfish inhabit the swamps and bayous of South Louisiana, encompassing the massive Atchafalaya Basin, the largest river drainage swamp in North America. More than ninety percent of all crawfish harvested in the United States comes from Louisiana, and much of it is consumed there.

The crustaceans are usually boiled live in a massive pot with a host of foods, such as onions, garlic, potatoes, sausage, corn, and artichokes. Cajun/Creole seasoning or seafood boil is added for flavor, along with bay leaves and cayenne pepper to taste. When all is thoroughly cooked, the crawfish and accoutrements are thrown on newspaper-lined tables in backyards and kitchens for what is known in Louisiana as the "crawfish boil."

To eat a crawfish, you first separate the head from the tail. Much like eating a lobster, the object is to remove the tail meat. The tail is pinched between two thumbs and the outer shell is removed leaving the tasty tail meat for consumption.

Some hearty souls enjoy sucking the rich flavorful fat and juices from the crawfish head. It is within the head that this fat can be culled for recipes. Packaged crawfish tails that are purchased in stores or on the Internet sometimes include the fat.

Bayou Benoit Crawfish Étouffée

Crawfish season usually begins in November and can last until mid-July in a good year. Everyone starts getting edgy around the beginning of fall as we await the first freshly caught tail meat. Étouffée literally means smothered, and we smother the crawfish in a nice gravy served over rice. However, this gravy is perfect for draping over a grilled rib-eye or filet mignon as well.

1 large onion, chopped
½ pound butter
½ cup crawfish fat
2 pounds Louisiana crawfish tail
   meat, peeled
2 teaspoons Cajun/Creole seasoning
1 tablespoon flour
¼ cup water
1 bunch parsley, chopped
1 bunch green onions, chopped
4 cups cooked Louisiana rice

SAUTÉ ONION in butter until translucent. Add crawfish fat, crawfish tails, and Cajun/Creole seasoning; stir and cover. Cook over medium heat for 15 to 20 minutes. Combine the flour and water to form a slurry and pour into the pot. Bring to a boil and turn off heat. Add parsley and green onions. Let sit for 10 to 15 minutes and then serve over cooked rice.

SERVES 6

Grand Bois Crawfish Boil

When I was a child in the 1960s, only poor people ate boiled crawfish. It was not something that city folks looked proudly upon or admitted to serving at home. Our Cajun family would travel to the levee where we would catch the tasty crustaceans and cook them at various camps and parks in the Atchafalaya Basin. Those city folks eventually realized what they were missing and now no one turns up their noses at a chance to attend a crawfish boil.

5 pounds small red potatoes
12 whole medium onions
12 small ears of corn on the cob
3 pounds smoked Cajun sausage
1½ cups crawfish/crab boil seasoning, divided
1 sack crawfish (40 to 45 pounds)

YOU WILL need two ice chests, a boiling basket for seafood and a pot large enough to hold the boiling basket for this recipe.

IN A large boiling pot, bring water to a boil and add potatoes and onions; boil for 15 minutes. Add corn and sausage and boil 5 minutes more. Remove from pot and place in first ice chest. Sprinkle ¼ cup seasoning evenly over top, then close ice chest and shake. Let stand for 15 minutes.

IN A large pot, bring water to a boil. Place crawfish in boiling basket and put in boiling water, cover. After steam appears around rim of cover wait 3 minutes and then remove the crawfish and place in second ice chest. Sprinkle remaining seasoning evenly over top, close ice chest and shake. Let sit for 15 minutes. Empty contents of both ice chests onto tables lined with newspaper.

SERVES 8

Peggy's Lounge Crawfish Bisque

Large family crawfish boils on the levee, park, or backyard inevitably result in leftovers. Many people purposely boil more crawfish than can be eaten by the assembled crowd in order to create more dishes. Peggy's Lounge in Cecilia sits less than a mile from the levee of the Atchafalaya Basin.

2 medium onions, chopped
1 large green bell pepper, chopped
1 stalk celery, chopped
2 sticks butter
2 cloves garlic, chopped
2 pounds crawfish tails, divided
1/4 cup breadcrumbs
5 teaspoons Cajun/Creole seasoning, divided
24 crawfish heads, cleaned
2 1/2 cups water
1/4 tablespoon roux (see page 28)
1 cup crawfish fat
1 bunch green onions, chopped
4 cups cooked Louisiana rice

PREHEAT OVEN to 350 degrees.

SAUTÉ THE onion, bell pepper, and celery in butter until tender. Add the garlic and sauté for a few minutes longer. Remove from heat. Coarsely chop 1 pound of the crawfish tail meat and mix in half of the sautéed vegetables and breadcrumbs. Season the mixture with 2 teaspoons Cajun/Creole seasoning. Stuff the mixture into the cleaned crawfish heads and bake at 350 degrees for 25 minutes; let cool.

IN A medium soup pot, bring the water to a boil and dissolve the roux. Add the crawfish fat, the remaining cooked vegetables and the remaining seasoning. Cook over medium heat for 15 minutes. Add the remaining crawfish tails and cook for 10 minutes. Add the stuffed heads and cook 10 minutes more. Remove from heat. Add green onions and let sit for 10 to 15 minutes. Serve over 1/2 cup cooked rice per serving.

SERVES 8

Tried-and-True Pecan Pie

This recipe is simple to make and always comes out beautifully to serve at the most important holidays and special events.

1 cup light corn syrup
3 eggs
1 cup sugar
2 tablespoons melted butter
1 teaspoon vanilla
1 (9-inch) pie shell
1 cup whole pecans
Vanilla ice cream

PREHEAT OVEN to 350 degrees.

MIX THE first five ingredients together thoroughly and pour into uncooked pie shell. Dot the top with the pecan halves until the top of the pie is covered in pecans. Bake on a cookie sheet on the middle shelf of the oven for about 45 minutes. The center of the pie should spring back when done. Let cool for 5 to 10 minutes before serving. Top with vanilla ice cream.

SERVES 8

CHAPTER 6 ✦ SOUTHWEST LOUISIANA

The southwestern corner of Louisiana, like most of the state, is home to a variety of nationalities, but the Cajun culture dominates in most areas. The culinary scene ranges from rice dishes from the rice fields to the east, to great seafood and wild game found on the coast and inland waterways to cattle raised throughout the prairie grasses.

Heading south from Lake Charles, it's a natural paradise. At any given time, travelers can spot numerous alligators, neo-tropical birds and rare *cheniers* on the Creole Nature Trail, where fishing, birding, crabbing, boating, and nature photography knows no limit. Southwest Louisiana lies within the Central and Mississippi Flyways for migrating birds, and some of the best places to view the more than three hundred

Among the southwest rice fields lies the town of Gueydan, considered the "Duck Capital of the World." More waterfowl visit Gueydan than any other area in the South, which is why Gueydan hosts an annual duck festival. According to Ducks Unlimited, Louisiana and neighbors Texas and Mississippi may witness 14 million ducks and 2 million geese flying through each winter.

bird species are the Cameron Prairie National Wildlife Refuge, Sam Houston Jones State Park, and the Sabine National Wildlife Refuge.

In addition to abundant waterfowl, birders may spot migrating warblers, roseate spoonbills, all varieties of egrets and herons, kingfishers, scarlet tanagers, orioles, white ibis, yellow-billed cuckoos, and many more.

But what people love most are the alligators. These giant reptiles became endangered in the early 1970s, and were protected from hunting for years. Today, alligators have made an amazing comeback and could quickly overpopulate the marshes if not for the annual alligator hunting season in September, which is strictly regulated by the state.

Among the southwest rice fields lies the town of Gueydan, considered the "Duck Capital of the World." More waterfowl visit Gueydan than any other area in the South, which is why Gueydan hosts an annual duck festival. According to *Ducks Unlimited*, Louisiana and neighbors Texas and Mississippi may witness 14 million ducks and 2 million geese flying through each winter.

Products created in the Southwest Cajun Country are Falcon rice products and Cajun Blast seasonings, sauces and rubs in Crowley, and Ragin' Cajun seasonings, relishes, marinades, and mixes produced in Lake Charles.

Egan Pumping Station Hen Gumbo

The fat from the browning process is used as the oil part of the roux—talk about good!

6 pounds chicken, cut into serving-size
  pieces with fat and skin left on
3/4 cup chicken fat oil (from browning
  the chicken)
1/4 cup cooking oil
1 1/4 cups flour
2 medium onions, chopped
1 large green bell pepper, chopped
1 stalk celery, chopped
1 gallon water
4 1/4 cups chicken broth or stock
1 pound tasso, cut into bite-size pieces
1 tablespoon Cajun/Creole seasoning
1 bunch green onions, chopped
1 bunch parsley, chopped
4 cups cooked Louisiana rice

BROWN HEN in a Dutch oven until golden brown and fat is rendered. Remove from pot. Add cooking oil and flour to the chicken fat and stir frequently until it turns a chocolate brown, about 30 minutes. Add onions, bell pepper, and celery, and sauté until vegetables are tender. Add hot water slowly, stirring to dissolve roux. Bring to a boil. Add chicken broth, tasso, and Cajun/Creole seasoning. Let cook, uncovered, over medium heat for 2 1/2 hours. Add green onions and parsley. Remove from heat. Serve in soup bowls over 1/2 cup cooked rice per serving.

SERVES 8

Grand Prairie Pork Backbone Fricassee

Hogs were raised in this part of Acadiana and shipped to New Orleans in order to provide a meat source for the growing metropolis. This pork recipe uses turnips, which add a depth of flavor that's hard to beat. No need to serve a dessert with this meal as it is very filling.

4 pounds pork fingers/country-style ribs
3 tablespoons cooking oil
1¼ cups chopped onions
¾ cup chopped green bell pepper
¾ cup chopped celery
4 tablespoons chopped garlic
4 cups chicken broth or stock
4 cups water
1 cup dark roux (see page 28)
5 teaspoons Cajun/Creole seasoning
4 tablespoons chicken base
6 medium turnips, cut in half
1 bunch green onions, chopped
4 cups cooked Louisiana rice

IN A heavy pot, brown pork in oil for 15 minutes and remove. Sauté vegetables until limp. Deglaze with broth and water. Add roux, Cajun/Creole seasoning, and chicken base, stirring to dissolve completely. Return meat to pot and cook over medium heat for 1½ hours. Add turnips and cook 20 minutes more. Remove from heat and add green onions. Serve over ½ cup cooked rice per serving.

SERVES 8

Cameron Parish Duck, Andouille, and Oyster Gumbo

When serving this recipe, the pot is normally cleaned with a couple of slices of bread by satisfied eaters.

$\frac{2}{3}$ cup cooking oil, divided

3 domestic ducks, cut and seasoned to taste

$1\frac{1}{3}$ cups rendered duck fat

$2\frac{1}{2}$ pounds andouille sausage

3 cups flour

$1\frac{1}{2}$ gallons water

1 gallon chicken broth or stock

1 cup chopped onion

1 cup chopped green bell pepper

1 cup chopped celery

1 cup chopped garlic

$2\frac{1}{2}$ pounds fresh sausage

2 tablespoons plus 2 teaspoons Cajun/Creole seasoning

$\frac{1}{2}$ cup chicken base

1 quart oysters, with liquid

1 bunch green onions, chopped

1 bunch parsley, chopped

6 cups cooked Louisiana rice

HEAT 2 tablespoons oil in a large Dutch oven. Place duck pieces in pot and brown while rendering fat for 30 minutes. Brown sausage for 3 minutes and remove both meats from pot. Add the remaining oil and flour and whisk briskly every 2 minutes for 30 minutes until it turns to a chocolate color. Add water and broth and bring to a boil. Place the onion, bell pepper, celery, and garlic in the liquid. Return the duck, andouille, and fresh sausage to the pot. Season with Cajun/Creole seasoning. Add chicken base and let cook for $2\frac{1}{2}$ hours over medium heat. Add oysters, green onions, and parsley. Remove from heat. Serve over $\frac{1}{2}$ cup cooked rice per serving.

SERVES 12

Iota Chicken and Fresh Sausage Gravy

Grandma could make a priest miss Sunday Mass with this rice and gravy dish.

2 tablespoons bacon grease
1 fryer chicken, cut into 8 pieces
2 pounds fresh sausage
2 medium onions, chopped
1 green bell pepper, chopped
2 teaspoons Cajun/Creole seasoning
3 cups chicken broth or stock
1½ cups water
1 bunch green onions, chopped
4 cups cooked Louisiana rice

ADD BACON grease to a heated Dutch oven. Add chicken to pot and sauté until golden brown. Remove chicken from pot. Add sausage whole and sauté until firm and browned on all sides. Remove sausage from pot and cut into 1-inch slices. Add onions, bell pepper, and Cajun/Creole seasoning to pot and sauté until vegetables are tender. Deglaze pot with broth and water. Return the chicken and sausage to pot and cook partially covered over medium heat for 1 hour. Turn off heat and add green onions. Let sit for 15 minutes. Serve in bowls with ½ cup cooked rice per serving.

SERVES 8

Lake Charles Chicken and Dumplings

This dish is the ultimate comfort food—especially for the kids!

GRAVY
4¼ cups chicken broth or stock
3 cups water
1 cup roux (see page 28)
5½-pound hen, cut into 12 pieces
2 medium onions, chopped
1 medium green bell pepper, chopped
1 stalk celery, chopped
2 bay leaves
4 teaspoons Cajun/Creole seasoning
1 bunch green onions, chopped
1 bunch parsley, chopped

DUMPLINGS
2 cups flour
2 tablespoons shortening
1 teaspoon baking powder
1 teaspoon Cajun/Creole seasoning

BRING BROTH and water to a boil in a large soup pot. Add roux and stir until completely dissolved. Add cut-up hen, onions, bell pepper, celery, bay leaves, and Cajun/Creole seasoning. Cover, leaving a small opening, and cook for 2½ hours over medium heat. Remove bay leaves. Add the green onions and parsley and stir.

FOR THE dumplings, mix the flour, shortening, baking powder, and Cajun/Creole seasoning. Drop into the soup pot with a tablespoon while the liquid is at a slight boil. Let cook, uncovered, for 10 minutes. Cover and let cook for 20 minutes over medium heat.

SERVES 8

Grand Lake Crab and Shrimp Boil

The absolutely best boiled crabs I ever had in my life came from a restaurant in Lake Charles, Louisiana. My crew and I had taped a show at Sam Houston Jones State Park and a vote was taken to decide what to eat for supper. Crabs won and so did we.

2 gallons water
1 cup Cajun-style seafood boil seasoning
  (can substitute with Old Bay seasoning)
1 stick butter
12 small red potatoes
2 cloves garlic
1 dozen live blue point crabs
6 ears fresh corn on the cob
2 pounds (26 to 30 count) Louisiana
  shrimp, heads on
10 pounds cubed ice

BRING WATER to a rolling boil in a deep outdoor-type boiling pot. Add seasoning, butter, potatoes, and garlic. Cook for 15 minutes, then add the crabs and corn on the cob to the pot and cover. Cook at a boil for 5 minutes. Add shrimp, cover, and cook at a boil for 5 minutes. Turn off heat and add ice to the pot. Let sit for 10 to 15 minutes before serving.

SERVES 6

Cajun Coleslaw

Cabbage grows almost all winter long in the temperate climate of South Louisiana. It is much easier to maintain than lettuce in our Southern latitude.

2 heads green cabbage, chopped
1 head purple cabbage, chopped
3 apples, chopped
1 pound carrots, shredded
3 cups mayonnaise
4 tablespoons honey
2 tablespoons cane or apple cider vinegar
Juice of 1 lemon
2 teaspoons Cajun/Creole seasoning

MIX THE cabbage, apples, and carrots together in a large bowl.

IN A separate bowl, combine the mayonnaise, honey, cane vinegar, lemon juice, and Cajun/Creole seasoning. Stir until completely mixed. Pour dressing over the cabbage mixture and fold together.

SERVES 10 AS A SIDE DISH

Hackberry Redfish with Tomatoes

The official license plate of Louisiana describes the state as "Sportsman's Paradise." There is a lot of truth to this claim! There is no other place in the U.S. where so many species of fish are available to harvest as off the coast of Louisiana. This redfish recipe pays tribute to one of the most exciting game fish in the Gulf of Mexico.

5 tablespoons olive oil
4 (8-ounce) redfish fillets
2 teaspoons Cajun/Creole seasoning, divided
2 tablespoons flour
1 large onion, chopped
1 small green bell pepper, julienned
2 cloves garlic, chopped
1 (28-ounce) can crushed tomatoes
2 bay leaves
1 teaspoon sugar
1 cup seafood stock
3 slices lemon
4 cups cooked Louisiana rice

PREHEAT OVEN to 350 degrees.

HEAT OLIVE oil in a Dutch oven on the stovetop. Sprinkle redfish fillets with enough Cajun/Creole seasoning to cover, and then dredge in flour. Brown fillets in oil over medium-high heat until golden brown, about 4 minutes each side. Remove fish from Dutch oven. Sauté the onion and bell pepper until tender. Add garlic and sauté for a couple of minutes. Add tomatoes, bay leaves, and sugar and cook for 10 minutes more, stirring often. Deglaze with stock and add remaining seasoning. Return fillets to pot. Place the lemon slices on top of fish. Cover and bake for 45 minutes. Serve over 1/2 cup cooked rice per serving.

SERVES 8

Sam Houston Jones Jambalaya

This State Park in Moss Bluff, Louisiana, is one of the most tranquil and eco-friendly places on the planet. If you are traveling through Louisiana, be sure to make this park a part of your itinerary.

3 pounds marinated pork
6 tablespoons cooking oil
1 pound rice dressing/stuffing mix
1¾ cups chopped onion
1 cup chopped green bell pepper
1 cup chopped celery
4 tablespoons chopped garlic
3 cups chicken broth or stock
3 tablespoons beef base
8 cups water
4 tablespoons Cajun/Creole seasoning
12 cups cooked Louisiana rice
½ bunch parsley, chopped
1 bunch green onions, chopped

IN A large heavy pot, brown marinated pork over high heat in oil for 20 to 30 minutes. Add dressing mix and continue to brown for 10 to 15 minutes. Add onion, bell pepper, celery, and garlic and sauté until soft. Deglaze with broth. Add beef base and water and stir to dissolve base. Add Cajun/Creole seasoning and cover, then cook over medium-high heat for 1½ hours, stirring occasionally. Remove from heat. Stir in cooked rice, parsley, and green onions.

SERVES 12

Baked Ducks Landry

This recipe works well for the "Old Tuesday Night Card Game" with the fellows.

4 ducks, skin on
1½ teaspoons Cajun/Creole seasoning
4 apples, quartered
4 pears, quartered
2 onions, quartered
3 tablespoons flour
¼ cup red wine

PREHEAT OVEN to 350 degrees.

SEASON DUCKS with Cajun/Creole seasoning and stuff cavities with apples, pears, and onions. Place in a large floured baking bag with red wine. Bake for 2 hours on baking pan. Serve immediately.

SERVES 4

Creole Garlic Butter Grilled Oysters

This is a life-altering dish! Beware of uncontrollable longings for this meal.

1 pound butter, melted
2 teaspoons garlic powder
1 teaspoon freshly squeezed lemon juice
2 teaspoons Cajun/Creole seasoning, divided
1 dozen oysters on the half shell

COMBINE THE butter, garlic powder, lemon juice, and 1 teaspoon Cajun/Creole seasoning together and place in a squeeze bottle. Place oysters on the half shell over the barbecue pit over very hot coals. Squeeze the sauce mixture generously on the oysters. The pit may flame so be careful. Cook, covered, for 10 to 12 minutes. Remove from pit and sprinkle remaining seasoning on the oysters.

SERVES 2

Gaspard Landing Étouffée

This étouffée recipe reflects the convergence of the swamp, sea, and farm by combining the different meats to create a dish that exemplifies the diversity of this part of Acadiana.

1 pound seasoned boneless chicken
2 tablespoons olive oil
2 sticks butter, divided
1 cup chopped onion
1/3 cup chopped green bell pepper
1/3 cup chopped celery
2 tablespoons chopped garlic
1 pound peeled Louisiana shrimp
1 pound peeled Louisiana crawfish
2 teaspoons Cajun/Creole seasoning
2 cups water
1 bunch green onions, chopped
5 cups cooked Louisiana rice

IN A large skillet, sauté the seasoned chicken in the oil and 3 tablespoons butter. Add onion, bell pepper, celery, garlic, and 1/2 stick butter and sauté until onions are transparent. Add the shrimp and sauté over high heat for 5 to 7 minutes. Add the crawfish (fat also) and 1/2 stick butter to pot, let cook for 5 minutes over high heat and season with Cajun/Creole seasoning. Deglaze with water and allow to cook down gradually, adding butter 1 tablespoon at a time as it becomes a gravy. Remove from heat and add the remaining butter and green onions to sauce. Serve over cooked rice.

SERVES 8

Basile Beet Salad

Canned beet salads provide a cool side dish to balance the spicy dishes of South Louisiana.

3 (15-ounce) cans sliced beets, drained
6 hard-boiled eggs, diced
½ white onion, sliced
¼ cup mayonnaise
1 teaspoon Cajun/Creole seasoning
1½ teaspoons sugar

MIX TOGETHER all of the ingredients in a large mixing bowl and refrigerate for 1 hour.

SERVES 8 AS A SIDE DISH

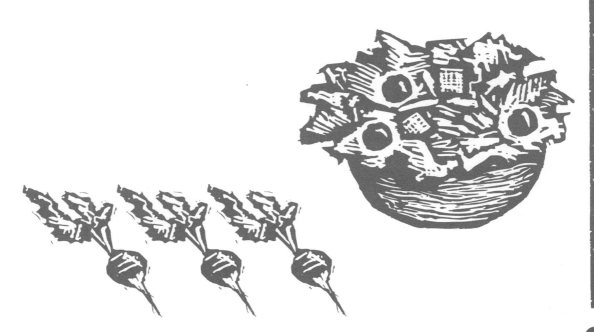

Butter Beans with Sausage

Butter beans are easy to grow and highly productive. The ability to dry them for future use adds to the value of the crop as a staple in our diet. Smoked meat and sausages add an incredible depth of flavor to this popular bean.

1 pound smoked sausage
3/4 cup chopped onion
1/2 cup chopped green bell pepper
1/2 cup chopped celery
4 tablespoons chopped garlic
3 tablespoons cooking oil
3 pounds frozen butter or lima beans
1 1/2 cups water
2 teaspoons Cajun/Creole seasoning
1 1/2 sticks butter
3 tablespoons sugar

CUTE THE sausage into bite-size pieces. Sauté the sausage, onion, bell pepper, celery, and garlic in oil until limp and slightly browned. Add beans, water, Cajun/Creole seasoning, butter, and sugar. Cook over medium heat for 1 hour, stirring occasionally. Remove 1 cup beans and smash into a paste and then return to pot.

SERVES 8

Sweet Potatoes Bayou Portage

If by chance you have leftovers, this makes a great ice cream topping.

1 pound pecans, toasted
1 stick butter, divided
1 (24-ounce) can yams or sweet
    potatoes, drained
1 (24-ounce) can yams or sweet
    potatoes, undrained
16 ounces fig preserves
2 teaspoons Cajun/Creole seasoning
4 tablespoons cane syrup

TOAST PECANS in a hot pan for 5 minutes. Add 1/2 stick butter. Add both cans of yams, fig preserves, Cajun/Creole seasoning, cane syrup, and remaining butter. Cook over medium heat for 35 to 40 minutes.

SERVES 8

Fried Eggplant Wheels

Eggplant is used extensively in recipes here in Cajun Country. The Spanish, Sicilian and Lebanese immigrants contributed a plethora of new ways to prepare this wonderful vegetable. This dish is often prepared as a side dish with fried fish.

2 medium eggplants, cut into
  ¼-inch slices
12 ounces sweetened condensed milk
1 teaspoon Cajun/Creole seasoning
16 ounces Cajun-style fish fry
2 quarts cooking oil

SOAK EGGPLANT in condensed milk and Cajun/ Creole seasoning. Dredge in fish fry, then fry in 350-degree oil until golden brown.

SERVES 6

Cajun Pain Perdue

This Cajun recipe for French toast warms up any child on a cold winter's day. Pain perdue translates to "lost bread" in English as stale bread was used to make this dish.

3 eggs
¾ cup milk
1 tablespoon brandy
1 teaspoon nutmeg
1 teaspoon vanilla
8 to 12 slices day-old French bread
  (not fresh or two days old)
5 tablespoons butter
Powdered sugar
Cane or maple syrup

BEAT THE eggs and then add the milk, brandy, nutmeg, and vanilla. Slice up the stale bread into thin slices and dip the pieces, both sides, into the egg mixture. Fry in the butter in a skillet over medium-low heat. When the pieces are toasted brown, remove from the skillet and top with powdered sugar. Serve with Louisiana cane syrup such as Steens or pure maple syrup.

SERVES 4-6

CHAPTER 7: MARSHES AND COAST

Some of the best fishing in America exists along the Cajun coast of Louisiana, from the eastern Grand Isle to Holly Beach in the west and every spot in between. ❧ At Grand Isle, fishermen routinely catch amberjack, drum, flounder, grouper, marlin, mackerel, redfish, snapper, swordfish, and tuna, to name a few, and excursions range from pier and surf casting to chartered services offshore. Almost every month there are fishing tournaments on the island. ❧ Other excellent fishing opportunities exist in Vermilion Bay, Cypremont Point, and along the Gulf at Cameron and Holly Beach. At Delcambre, shrimp reins supreme.

Outside of its seafood bounty, the Cajun coastline and inland marshes include towns such as Franklin with its numerous historic properties, a wide variety of state parks and campgrounds, plantation homes, swamp tours, and the Chitimacha Indian Museum, to name a few. More than sixteen fairs and festivals occur along the Cajun Coast, including the popular Shrimp and Petroleum Festival every Labor Day in Morgan City.

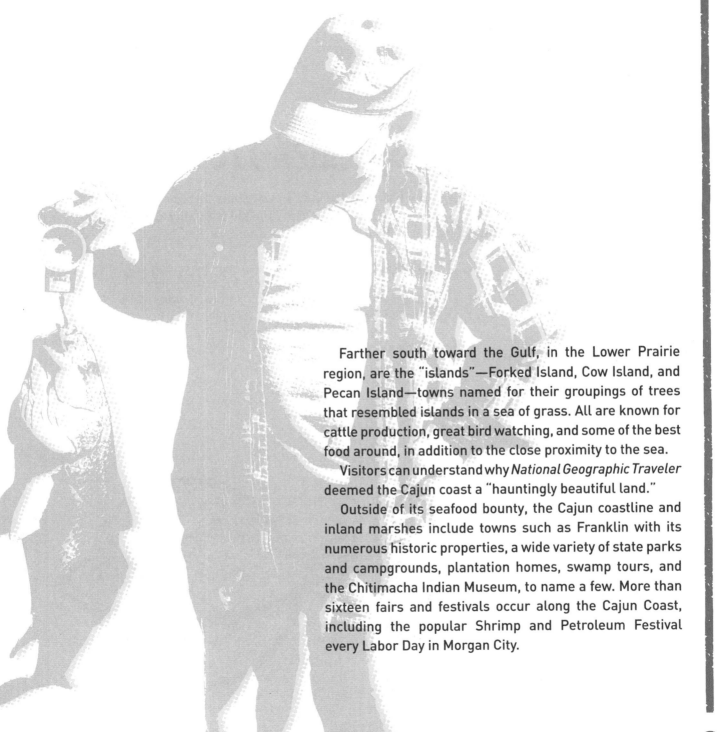

Farther south toward the Gulf, in the Lower Prairie region, are the "islands"—Forked Island, Cow Island, and Pecan Island—towns named for their groupings of trees that resembled islands in a sea of grass. All are known for cattle production, great bird watching, and some of the best food around, in addition to the close proximity to the sea.

Visitors can understand why *National Geographic Traveler* deemed the Cajun coast a "hauntingly beautiful land."

Outside of its seafood bounty, the Cajun coastline and inland marshes include towns such as Franklin with its numerous historic properties, a wide variety of state parks and campgrounds, plantation homes, swamp tours, and the Chitimacha Indian Museum, to name a few. More than sixteen fairs and festivals occur along the Cajun Coast, including the popular Shrimp and Petroleum Festival every Labor Day in Morgan City.

Cypremont Point Speckled Trout

Speckled trout is arguably the finest eating fish from the Gulf. In Louisiana, the limit is 25 per person and on a good day you can catch a limit in an hour. The fall is usually the best time of the year to go fishing for trout, but speckled trout are around all year long.

10 speckled trout fillets
4 teaspoons Cajun/Creole seasoning
5 eggs, beaten
1½ cups milk
3 tablespoons mustard
3 pounds corn flour, seasoned
1 gallon cooking oil

SEASON FISH fillets with Cajun/Creole seasoning. Mix the eggs, milk, and mustard together, then add the fish. Let stand for 15 minutes. Dredge marinated fish in seasoned corn flour and fry for 7 minutes submerged in oil. Serve hot.

SERVES 6

Mermentau Stuffed Sunday Pork Roast

At our family supermarket, Breaux's Mart, we sell massive amounts of pork roast on rainy weekends. My brother, Wally Breaux, is the butcher at our store, a demanding job requiring 80-hour weeks under stressful conditions. I could never fill his shoes and be that committed.

STUFFING
¼ cup chopped onion
3 tablespoons chopped bell pepper
3 tablespoons chopped garlic
2 tablespoons fresh cayenne pepper
1½ tablespoons Cajun/Creole seasoning
2 tablespoons vinegar

ROAST WITH GRAVY
5-pound pork roast (butt or shoulder works well)
4 tablespoons cooking oil
2 medium onions, chopped
1 medium green bell pepper, chopped
1 stalk celery, chopped
2 teaspoons Cajun/Creole seasoning
1 (15-ounce) can beef broth
4 cups water
½ bunch parsley, chopped
½ bunch green onions, chopped
4 cups cooked Louisiana rice

TO MAKE the stuffing, mix all ingredients together and let sit for 30 minutes.

TO MAKE the roast, cut ¼-inch-wide x ½-inch deep slits in roast in 15 to 20 different places and fill with stuffing. Heat oil in a Dutch oven on the stovetop. Place roast in pot and brown on all sides over medium-high heat until golden brown. Remove roast. Add onions, bell pepper, celery, and Cajun/Creole seasoning and sauté until tender and browning starts to occur. Deglaze with the broth, scraping bottom of pot to release brown bits. Add water and return roast to pot. Cook over medium heat, covered, for 3 hours, turning roast over every 30 minutes. Add parsley and green onions and stir into gravy. Serve over ½ cup cooked rice per serving.

SERVES 8

Grand Chenier Crawfish Jambalaya

This is old school Cajun cooking. The crawfish fat adds a level of flavor that is impossible to duplicate with any other ingredient.

2 medium onions, chopped
1 medium green bell pepper, chopped
1 stalk celery, chopped
½ pound butter
2 cloves garlic, chopped
1 cup crawfish fat
2 tablespoons roux (see page 28)
2½ teaspoons Cajun/Creole seasoning
2 cups seafood stock
2 pounds crawfish tails, peeled
1 bunch green onions, chopped
5 cups cooked Louisiana rice

OVER MEDIUM heat, sauté the onions, bell pepper, and celery in butter until soft. Add garlic and sauté for 3 to 5 minutes. Be careful not to brown. Add crawfish fat, roux, Cajun/Creole seasoning, and stock. Stir until roux is completely dissolved. Cook over medium heat for 35 to 40 minutes. Turn off heat and add crawfish tails and green onions. Slowly incorporate rice into pot, stirring until well mixed.

SERVES 6

Shell Beach Green Gumbo

This nourishing and hearty soup is not widely prepared in Acadiana. We know of only one restaurant located in Carencro, Louisiana, that lists it on the menu. This recipe is from Pete Hebert, whose wife is from the Charenton area next to the Chitimacha nation. He said his mother-in-law used to fix green gumbo when he was courting his wife back in the late 1940s.

4 cups water
3 cups chicken stock or broth
1 cup dark roux (see page 28)
2 pounds Cajun-style smoked sausage,
  cut into 1-inch slices
1 large onion, chopped
1 medium green bell pepper, chopped
1 stalk celery, finely chopped
2 cloves garlic, chopped
8 cups mustard greens, washed and cut
4 teaspoons Cajun/Creole seasoning
1 bunch green onions, chopped
1 bunch parsley, chopped
5 cups cooked Louisiana rice

BRING WATER and stock to a boil in a large soup pot. Completely dissolve roux in liquid. Add sausage, onion, bell pepper, celery, garlic, mustard greens, and Cajun/Creole seasoning. Cook over medium heat for 45 minutes. Remove from heat. Add the green onions and parsley. Cover and let sit for 15 minutes. Serve over ½ cup cooked rice per serving.

SERVES 10

Gibbstown Bridge Deer Backstrap

This is the filet mignon section of the deer that's best served medium rare. This dish is normally served on special occasions, as the backstrap is the finest part of the venison and not readily available.

6 (12-ounce) venison steaks
  (or substitute beef tenderloin steaks)
1 tablespoon olive oil
1 (3.4-ounce) bottle Montreal Steak
  Seasoning

PREHEAT OVEN to 450 degrees.

SEAR MEAT on all sides in oil in a hot skillet until browned. Season liberally with steak seasoning and bake for 10 to 12 minutes. Let stand for 7 minutes and serve.

SERVES 6

Pecan Island Catfish Étouffée

This is the Cajun idea of fast food. The dish can be prepared in 40 minutes and is perfect for a family supper at the camp. Make sure not to overcook the catfish as it will fall apart into small pieces.

2 large onions, chopped
1 large green bell pepper, chopped
2¹/₂ sticks butter, divided
2 cloves garlic, chopped
2 teaspoons Cajun/Creole seasoning
1 cup seafood stock
3 pounds catfish fillets
1 bunch green onions, chopped
¹/₂ bunch parsley, chopped
5 cups cooked Louisiana rice

SAUTÉ THE onions and bell pepper in 2 sticks butter until soft. Add garlic and Cajun/Creole seasoning and sauté for a few minutes. Do not brown garlic. Add stock and cook over medium heat until reduced by half. Place catfish fillets in sauce and cook over medium heat for 20 minutes. Remove from heat. Add the remaining butter and stir to dissolve. Add the green onions and parsley. Serve over cooked rice.

SERVES 8

Johnson Bayou Flame-Kissed Rib-Eyes

Surf and turf never had it so good!

8 (1-inch-thick) rib-eye steaks
5 tablespoons Montreal Steak Seasoning

OVER VERY hot coals (should flame up as fat melts), cook steaks for 8 to 10 minutes on each side. Alternate directions of steaks, twice on each side to create a crisscrossed design. Season with Montreal seasoning at the last minute on the grill.

SERVES 8

Alligator Sauce Piquante in Creole Louisiana

I journey to Creole, Louisiana, every September to participate in the alligator hunt on the Miami Corporation land. The fierce independence of the inhabitants of the area is a trait that reminds me of the pioneers of the past. I would hunt with Old Fats Dupont and in the evening cook meals for a rowdy bunch of fellows in some pretty primitive camps along the coastal area of Cameron Parish. Old Fats is gone now, but if I close my eyes I can still see his smile and hear his thundering voice. This was a meal that he particularly loved.

2 (8-ounce) cans tomato paste
¾ cup chopped onion
½ cup chopped green bell pepper
½ cup chopped celery
4 tablespoons chopped garlic
2 teaspoons sugar
1 (16-ounce) can tomato puree
3 (8-ounce) cans tomato sauce
2 (15-ounce) cans diced tomatoes,
  including liquid
6 cups chicken stock or broth
3 tablespoons chicken base
2 tablespoons seafood base
5 teaspoons Cajun/Creole seasoning
4 pounds alligator, cut into bite-size
  pieces (ask your grocer to order if
  not available)
3 pounds medium shrimp
6 cups cooked Louisiana rice

BROWN TOMATO paste for 12 minutes in a stockpot over high heat. Add onion, bell pepper, celery, and garlic, and sauté until limp. Add sugar, tomato puree, tomato sauce, tomatoes, stock, chicken base, seafood base, and Cajun/Creole seasoning, then stir and cook over medium heat for 1½ hours. Add the alligator and cook for 40 minutes. Add shrimp and cook 15 minutes more. Serve over ½ cup cooked rice per serving.

SERVES 12

Lake Misere Corn and Crab Soup

In the coastal areas of Acadiana, we go crabbing on the side of the road in the brackish canals that parallel the roadways. The tackle required consists of a string, fresh turkey neck, and a net. Make sure to have a current Louisiana fishing license.

1 stick butter
1 medium onion, finely chopped
¼ cup flour
2 cups seafood stock
3 teaspoons Cajun/Creole seasoning
¼ teaspoon nutmeg
2 cups half-and-half
1 cup heavy or whipping cream
1 pound fresh or frozen whole kernel corn
2 (15-ounce) cans cream-style corn
1 pound crabmeat (claw)
1 pound lump crabmeat
1 bunch green onions, chopped
French bread, optional

MELT THE butter in a large soup pot over medium-low heat. Add the onion and sauté until tender. Do not brown butter. Add the flour and cook until a blond roux forms. Add the stock, Cajun/Creole seasoning, and nutmeg, and stir to dissolve roux. Add half-and-half, cream, whole kernel corn, and cream-style corn, and cook over medium-high heat for 15 to 20 minutes. Add crabmeat and green onions. Stir and remove from heat. Let sit for 10 minutes. Serve in soup bowls with crusty French bread on the side, if desired.

SERVES 8

Redfish Point Oyster Cornbread Dressing

This is one of the easiest and possibly one of the best oyster recipes. It is usually served as a side dish with baked fish.

1½ sticks butter
1 bunch green onions, finely chopped
2 pints chopped oysters with oyster liquid
1½ teaspoons Cajun/Creole seasoning
1½ pounds cooked cornbread, crumbled

MELT THE butter in a saucepan. Sauté white part of green onions until limp. Add oysters with liquid and Cajun/Creole seasoning and heat through. Remove from heat and add cornbread to mixture. Add the remaining green onions and stir.

SERVES 6 AS A SIDE DISH

Moss Bluff Oyster Bisque

I love to go fishing at the Hackberry Rod and Gun Club in western Acadiana. My friend, Mike Chachere, and I travel there quite often to catch a limit of speckled trout and redfish. We are often back in a couple of hours with all we can keep. The fishing guides there really know how to cook and this is one dish I'm fairly fond of.

1 large onion, finely chopped
1 carrot, finely chopped
1 celery stalk, finely chopped
2 teaspoons butter
1 teaspoon olive oil
2 teaspoons flour
2 cups half-and-half
1 cup heavy cream
2 teaspoons Cajun/Creole seasoning
¼ teaspoon nutmeg
1 quart oysters, with oyster liquid
½ bunch parsley, chopped

SAUTÉ THE onion, carrot, and celery in the butter and oil over medium heat until tender. Add flour and cook for 3 to 4 minutes until a blond roux forms. Add the half-and-half, cream, Cajun/Creole seasoning, and nutmeg. Stir until roux is dissolved. Cook for 5 minutes over medium heat. Do not boil. Add oysters with liquid. Remove from heat and add parsley. Serve in soup bowls with crackers on the side.

SERVES 6

Declouet Highway Beef Tongue—Sherman's Camp

The tongue takes about 4 hours to cook, but the resulting gravy and tender meat is worth every second of effort.

1¾ cups finely chopped onions, divided
1¾ cups finely chopped green bell peppers, divided
2 tablespoons finely chopped garlic
2½ teaspoons Cajun/Creole seasoning, divided
2 small beef tongues
4 tablespoons cooking oil
1 (15-ounce) can chicken broth
3 cups water
1½ tablespoons beef base
1 bunch green onions, chopped
4 cups cooked Louisiana rice

MIX TOGETHER ¼ cup onion, ¼ cup bell pepper, garlic, and 1 teaspoon Cajun/Creole seasoning. Cut 10 to 12 slits in each tongue, about 1 x 2 x 1-inch lengths, and fill the slits with the stuffing mixture.

IN A heavy pot, brown tongues in oil until very brown, about 25 minutes. Add remaining onions and bell peppers and sauté until soft. Add broth and sauté until a paste forms. Add water, beef base, and remaining seasoning and cook over low heat for 3½ hours, stirring occasionally. Add green onions, turn off heat and stir. Serve over ½ cup cooked rice per serving.

SERVES 8

Nu-Nu's Shrimp Stew with Boiled Eggs

In South Louisiana, terms of endearment or nicknames are often used, with some people receiving a few unique ones. My grandpa called me Nu-Nu all of his life. Grandpa loved this recipe for shrimp stew. He made sure to save some for the next day's lunch.

2 gallons water
4 (8-ounce) jars clam juice
2 cups roux (see page 28)
1¾ cups chopped onion
1 cup chopped green bell pepper
1 cup chopped celery
4 tablespoons chopped garlic
3 (¾-ounce) packs dried shrimp powder
1½ tablespoons Cajun/Creole seasoning
5 pounds peeled shrimp
2 dozen hard-boiled eggs, peeled
1 bunch parsley, chopped
2 bunches green onions, chopped
12 cups cooked Louisiana rice

IN A deep pot, combine the water and clam juice and bring to a boil. Add the roux, stirring until completely dissolved. Add the vegetables, shrimp powder, and Cajun/Creole seasoning and cook over medium heat for 45 minutes (liquid should reduce by one-third). Add shrimp and whole, peeled eggs and cook for 15 minutes. Remove from heat. Add the parsley and green onions. Let sit, covered, for 30 minutes. Serve over ½ cup cooked rice per serving.

SERVES 24

Louisiana Gulf Shrimp and Tasso Shish Kebabs

What better way to spend a summer afternoon than feasting on such a delightful meal with friends and family. This really marries well with a chilled bottle of Pinot Grigio and good conversation.

2 purple onions, cut into 1-inch chunks
2 green bell peppers, cut into
   1-inch chunks
1 pound tasso, cut into 1 x ¼-inch pieces
   (or substitute smoked ham)
1 pint cherry tomatoes
1 pound medium shrimp, peeled
2 teaspoons Cajun/Creole seasoning

PLACE THE ingredients on 8 shish kebab skewers in this pattern: onion, bell pepper, tasso, tomato, 3 shrimp, tasso, onion, bell pepper, 2 shrimp, tasso, tomato, onion, bell pepper. Season with the Cajun/Creole seasoning and grill on hot coals for 10 minutes, turning occasionally.

SERVES 8

Berwick Onion Rings Rice Pilaf

This rice dish is somewhat like paella, but without the seafood. The dishes such as this one illustrate the continuing impact of the Spanish culture in our cuisine.

4 cups cooked rice
1 pound frozen sweet peas
1 (10-ounce) can fried onion rings
1 (12-ounce) can cooked carrots
8 ounces cooked ham, cubed
1 bunch green onions, sliced
2 teaspoons Cajun/Creole seasoning
1 cup chicken broth
2 tablespoons butter

COMBINE ALL the ingredients in a foil bag and place on a barbecue pit for 25 to 30 minutes.

SERVES 6

Sherman's Camp Style Cabbage

Cabbage does well in South Louisiana in the fall until January, and again in the spring until May.

1 pound tasso, diced (or substitute ham)
1 tablespoon cooking oil
1 medium yellow onion, sliced
1½ cups chicken broth or stock
2 heads green cabbage, cut into chunks
1 teaspoon Cajun/Creole seasoning

BROWN THE tasso in the oil. Add the onion and sauté until tender. Deglaze pan with the chicken broth. Add cabbage and Cajun/Creole seasoning. Cook over medium heat for 35 to 40 minutes, stirring often.

SERVES 6

Marsh Island Crab, Shrimp, and Okra Gumbo

The winter is dismal in the Atchafalaya Basin with the endless grey skies and the thick humidity combined to create a melancholy deep in one's soul. The only cure and comfort comes in a bowl of gumbo shared with family and friends. The fishermen, hunters, and farmers of the swamp have mastered the slow cooking method required to produce these fulfilling cold weather dishes.

¼ cup cooking oil
4 pounds okra, sliced ¼-inch thick
2 tablespoons white vinegar
5 teaspoons Cajun/Creole seasoning, divided
5¼ cups water
4¼ cups seafood stock
½ cup roux (see page 28)
6 whole gumbo crabs, cleaned
1 (6-ounce) can crabmeat
1 large onion, chopped
1 medium green bell pepper, chopped
1 stalk celery, chopped
2 pounds medium shrimp, cleaned and deveined
1 pound crabmeat (claw)
1 pound lump white crabmeat
8 cups cooked Louisiana rice

HEAT THE oil in a heavy gauge pan. Add the okra, vinegar, and 2 teaspoons Cajun/Creole seasoning. Cook for 1 hour, covered, over medium heat, stirring to prevent scorching. Remove from heat and set aside.

BRING THE water and stock to a boil in a large soup pot. Add the roux and stir to dissolve. Add whole gumbo crabs, crabmeat, onion, bell pepper, celery, and remaining seasoning. Cook over medium heat for 1 hour and 15 minutes uncovered (stock will reduce considerably). Add cooked okra and shrimp and cook for 15 to 20 minutes. Add crabmeat and cook 5 minutes more. Remove from heat. Serve in soup bowls over ½ cup cooked rice per serving.

SERVES 16

Southwest Pass Turnips

You have never eaten turnips if you have not had them prepared this way.

8 turnips, peeled
¼ cup cane syrup
⅛ cup Tiger Sauce (or hot sauce)
½ stick butter

STEAM PEELED turnips for 30 minutes, or until fork tender. Heat the cane syrup, Tiger Sauce, and butter in a separate pan to a slow boil, and then pour over cooked turnips.

SERVES 8

Dark Sugar Pralines

These pralines turn out darker than most because of the brown sugar, but they're creamy as well. Humidity will affect the consistency of pralines. Humid Louisiana summers, for instance, can sometimes cause gooey pralines that don't harden well.

3 cups packed brown sugar
1 cup evaporated milk or whipping cream
2 tablespoons corn syrup
½ teaspoon salt
½ cup butter
2 cups pecans
1¼ teaspoons vanilla

IN A large saucepan over medium heat, mix the brown sugar, milk, corn syrup, and salt. Bring to a boil, stirring constantly. Once a boil has been reached, cook until a candy thermometer reads 234 degrees, stirring occasionally. Remove from heat and add the butter but do not stir. Cool until candy thermometer reads 150 degrees, about 35 minutes. Stir in pecans and vanilla with a wooden spoon until candy thickens and butter and vanilla are well absorbed but still glossy, about 5 to 7 minutes. Quickly drop onto wax paper in patties. Allow to cool.

MAKES ABOUT 30 MEDIUM PRALINES

Food Festivals in Cajun Country

ALLIGATOR FESTIVAL
Luling
www.stcharlesrotary.com/
alligatorfestival.htm

ATCHAFALAYA CATFISH FESTIVAL
Melville
www.cajuntravel.com/festivals

BOUDIN COOK-OFF
Lafayette
www.boudincookoff.com

GHEENS BON MANGÉ FESTIVAL
Gheens

BREAUX BRIDGE CRAWFISH FESTIVAL
Breaux Bridge
www.bbcrawfest.com

CATFISH FESTIVAL
Des Allemands

CATFISH FESTIVAL
Washington
townofwashingtonla.org

CRACKLIN FESTIVAL
Port Barre

DELCAMBRE SHRIMP FESTIVAL
Delcambre
www.shrimpfestival.net

ÉTOUFFÉE FESTIVAL
Arnaudville
www.cajuntravel.com/festivals

FESTIVALS ACADIENS ET CRÉOLES
Lafayette
www.festivalsacadiens.com

FRENCH FOOD FESTIVAL
Larose
www.bayoucivicclub.org

FROG FESTIVAL
Rayne
http://rayne.org

GIANT OMELETTE CELEBRATION
Abbeville
www.giantomelette.org

GUEYDAN DUCK FESTIVAL
Gueydan
www.duckfestival.org

INTERNATIONAL RICE FESTIVAL
Crowley
www.ricefestival.com

JAMBALAYA FESTIVAL
Gonzales
www.jambalayafestival.org

LOUISIANA CATTLE FESTIVAL
Abbeville

LOUISIANA GUMBO FESTIVAL
Chackbay
www.lagumbofest.com

LOUISIANA SUGAR CANE FESTIVAL
New Iberia
www.hisugar.org

LOUISIANA YAMBILEE FESTIVAL
Opelousas
www.yambilee.com

Cajun Food Websites

OLD TIME BOUCHERIE
Eunice

OPELOUSAS SPICE AND MUSIC FESTIVAL
Opelousas
www.opelousasspiceandmusic
festival.com/

PEPPER FESTIVAL
St. Martinville
www.stmartinkiwanis.org

PRAIRIE CAJUN FOLKLIFE FESTIVAL
Eunice

ST. JOHN ANDOUILLE FESTIVAL
LaPlace
www.stjohnla.us/andouillefestival.
asp

SHRIMP AND PETROLEUM FESTIVAL
Morgan City
www.shrimp-petrofest.org

SMOKED MEAT FESTIVAL/LA FESTIVALE DE LA VIANDE BOUCANÉE
Ville Platte
www.smokedmeatfestival.com

SORRENTO BOUCHERIE FESTIVAL
Sorrento
www.eatel.net/~fred/boucherie/

WORLD CHAMPIONSHIP CRAWFISH ÉTOUFFÉE COOKOFF
Eunice
www.eunice-la.com/festivals.html

"CAJUN" KARL BREAUX
www.cajunkarl.com

BOUDIN LINK
www.boudinlink.com

BOURQUE'S SUPERSTORE
www.bourquespecialties.com

BRUCE FOODS
www.brucefoods.com

CAJUN BLAST
www.cajunblast.com

CAJUN MICROWAVE
www.cajunmicrowaves.com

CAJUN POWER SAUCES
www.cajunpowersauce.com

CAJUN SUPERMARKET
www.cajunsupermarket.com

FALCON RICE MILL
www.falconrice.com

Cajun Tourism Websites

CHEF JOHN FOLSE
www.jfolse.com

HEBERT'S SPECIALTY MEATS
www.hebertsmeats.com

KONRICO RICE
www.conradricemill.com

LOUISIANA SEAFOOD PROMOTION AND MARKETING BOARD
www.louisianaseafood.com

MELLO JOY
www.mellojoy.com

RAGIN' CAJUN FOODS
www.ragincajunfoods.com

SAVOIE'S
www.savoiesfoods.com

SLAP YA MAMA
www.slapyamama.com

SOUTHERN FOODWAYS ALLIANCE BOUDIN TRAIL
www.southernboudintrail.com

STEENS
www.steensyrup.com

SUIRE'S
www.suires.oldnewbie.net

TABASCO
www.tabasco.com

TONY CHACHERE'S
www.tonychachere.com

ACADIA PARISH TOURIST COMMISSION
www.acadiatourism.org

ACADIAN MUSEUM
www.acadianmuseum.com

CAJUN COAST
www.cajuncoast.com

CAMERON PARISH TOURIST COMMISSION
www.cameronparishtourist commission.org

CENTER FOR CULTURAL AND ECO-TOURISM, UNIVERSITY OF LOUISIANA AT LAFAYETTE
ccet.louisiana.edu/tourism-cultural.html

CREOLE NATURE TRAIL
www.creolenaturetrail.org

EVANGELINE PARISH TOURIST COMMISSION
www.evangelinetourism.com

Bibliography

GRAND ISLE TOURIST COMMISSION
www.grand-isle.com

**HOUMA CONVENTION AND
VISITORS BUREAU**
www.houmatravel.com

**IBERIA PARISH CONVENTION
AND VISITOR'S BUREAU**
www.iberiatravel.com

**JEAN LAFITTE NATIONAL HISTORICAL
PARK AND PRESERVE**
www.nps.gov/jela

**JEFFERSON DAVIS PARISH
TOURIST COMMISSION**
www.jeffdavis.org

**LAFAYETTE CONVENTION AND
VISITOR'S COMMISSION**
www.lafayettetravel.com

**LAFOURCHE PARISH
TOURIST COMMISSION**
www.visitlafourche.com

LOUISIANA TOURISM
www.louisianatravel.com

SAVOY'S MUSIC CENTER
www.savoymusiccenter.com

ST. LANDRY PARISH
www.cajuntravel.com

**ST. MARTIN PARISH
TOURIST COMMISSION**
www.cajuncountry.org

**SOUTHWEST LOUISIANA CONVENTION
AND VISITOR'S BUREAU**
www.visitlakecharles.org

VERMILION PARISH TOURISM
www.vermilion.org

Bienvenu, Marcelle, Carl A. Brasseaux, and Ryan A. Brasseaux. 2005. *Stir the Pot: The History of Cajun Cuisine.* New York: Hippocrene Books.

Brasseaux, Carl. 1987. *The Founding of New Acadia: The Beginnings of Acadian Life in Louisiana, 1765–1803.* Baton Rouge, La.: Louisiana State University Press.

Feibleman, Peter S. 1971. *American Cooking: Creole and Acadian.* New York: Time-Life Books.

Wohl, Kit. 2005. *Arnaud's Restaurant Cookbook.* Gretna, La.: Pelican Publishing Company.

Index